DATE DUE

OC 22 02			
FE 9 06			

DEMCO 38-296

Taxing Multinational Corporations

A National Bureau
of Economic Research
Project Report

Taxing Multinational Corporations

Edited by   Martin Feldstein,
James R. Hines, Jr.,
and R. Glenn Hubbard

The University of Chicago Press

Chicago and London

Taxing multinational
corporations

the George F. Baker Professor of Economics at Har-
resident of the National Bureau of Economic Re-
ᴇꜱ, Jʀ., is associate professor of public policy at the
᷍᷍᷍᷍᷍ol of Government of Harvard University and a
faculty research fellow of the National Bureau of Economic Research.
R. Gʟᴇɴɴ Hᴜʙʙᴀʀᴅ is the Russell L. Carson Professor of Economics
and Finance at the Graduate School of Business of Columbia University
and a research associate of the National Bureau of Economic Research.

The University of Chicago Press, Chicago 60637
The University of Chicago Press, Ltd., London
© 1995 by The National Bureau of Economic Research
All rights reserved. Published 1995
Printed in the United States of America
04 03 02 01 00 99 98 97 96 95 1 2 3 4
ISBN: 0-226-24094-0 (cloth)

Library of Congress Cataloging-in-Publication Data

Taxing multinational corporations / edited by Martin Feldstein, James
  Hines, and R. Glenn Hubbard.
        p.   cm.—(A National Bureau of Economic Research project
  report)
    Includes bibliographical references and index.
    1. International business enterprises—Taxation. 2. Corporations,
  American—Taxation.   I. Feldstein, Martin S.   II. Hines, James R.
  III. Hubbard, R. Glenn.   IV. Series
  HD2753.A3T388   1995
  336.24′3—dc20   95–2789
                                                             CIP

Relation of the Directors to the
Work and Publications of the
National Bureau of Economic Research

1. The object of the National Bureau of Economic Research is to ascertain and to present to the public important economic facts and their interpretation in a scientific and impartial manner. The board of Directors is charged with the responsibility of ensuring that the work of the National Bureau is carried on in strict conformity with this object.

2. The President of the National Bureau shall submit to the Board of Directors, or to its Executive Committee, for their formal adoption all specific proposals for research to be instituted.

3. No research report shall be published by the National Bureau until the President has sent each member of the Board a notice that a manuscript is recommended for publication and that in the President's opinion it is suitable for publication in accordance with the principles of the National Bureau. Such notification will include an abstract or summary of the manuscript's content and a response form for use by those Directors who desire a copy of the manuscript for review. Each manuscript shall contain a summary drawing attention to the nature and treatment of the problem studied, the character of the data and their utilization in the report, and the main conclusions reached.

4. For each manuscript so submitted, a special committee of the Directors (including Directors Emeriti) shall be appointed by majority agreement of the President and Vice Presidents (or by the Executive Committee in case of inability to decide on the part of the President and Vice Presidents), consisting of three Directors selected as nearly as may be one from each general division of the Board. The names of the special manuscript committee shall be stated to each Director when notice of the proposed publication is submitted to him. It shall be the duty of each member of the special manuscript committee to read the manuscript. If each member of the manuscript committee signifies his approval within thirty days of the transmittal of the manuscript, the report may be published. If at the end of that period any member of the manuscript committee withholds his approval, the President shall then notify each member of the Board, requesting approval or disapproval of publication, and thirty days additional shall be granted for this purpose. The manuscript shall then not be published unless at least a majority of the entire Board who shall have voted on the proposal within the time fixed for the receipt of votes shall have approved.

5. No manuscript may be published, though approved by each member of the special manuscript committee, until forty-five days have elapsed from the transmittal of the report in manuscript form. The interval is allowed for the receipt of any memorandum of dissent or reservation, together with a brief statement of his reasons, that any member may wish to express; and such memorandum of dissent or reservation shall be published with the manuscript if he so desires. Publication does not, however, imply that each member of the Board has read the manuscript, or that either members of the Board in general or the special committee has passed on its validity in every detail.

6. Publications of the National Bureau issued for informational purposes concerning the work of the Bureau and its staff, or issued to inform the public of activities of Bureau staff, and volumes issued as a result of various conferences involving the National Bureau shall contain a specific disclaimer noting that such publication has not passed through the normal review procedures required in this resolution. The Executive Committee of the Board is charged with review of all such publications from time to time to ensure that they do not take on the character of formal research reports of the National Bureau, requiring formal Board approval.

7. Unless otherwise determined by the Board or exempted by the terms of paragraph 6, a copy of this resolution shall be printed in each National Bureau publication.

(Resolution adopted October 25, 1926, as revised through September 30, 1974)

Contents

Preface

The tax treatment of multinational corporations is as important as it is complex. Those who analyze the effects of taxes on American multinational companies must look at the U.S. tax rules, at foreign rules, and at their interaction. Many tax laws that are written with the domestic economy in mind nevertheless have substantial effects on American companies that invest abroad or do business abroad.

The papers in this volume are intended to discuss some of these important issues in a relatively nontechnical way. They were prepared for a conference in Washington, DC, in April 1994. The research summarized in these papers was presented at an earlier conference for NBER researchers and other economists that was held in Cambridge, MA, in January 1994. Those papers are available in a separate volume, *The Effects of Taxation on Multinational Corporations* (University of Chicago Press, 1995), which we edited.

This research is part of an ongoing series of studies that NBER researchers have been doing for several years and that have been published in several previous NBER volumes. The studies in the present volume deal with a wide variety of issues, including the effects of tax rules on U.S. competitiveness, on the volume and location of R&D spending, on the extent of foreign direct investment, and on the financial practices of multinational companies. The introduction to this volume summarizes the major findings of the chapters that follow.

The research presented here has benefited from frequent interaction among the members of the research project and from the opportunity to discuss the research at earlier stages with a wider group of economists interested in international tax issues as well as with corporate tax lawyers and Treasury Department staff.

We are grateful to the U.S. Treasury Department for making unpublished data available to the research group and for the opportunity to collaborate with members of the Treasury staff. Funding that made this project possible was provided by the Ford Foundation, the Bradley Foundation, the Starr Foundation, and several multinational corporations. The funds for the Washington conference were provided by the Ford Foundation.

We are grateful to the members of the NBER staff for their assistance with all of the details involved in the planning and execution of this research and of the many meetings that took place along the way. In addition to the researchers and research assistants named in the individual papers, we are grateful to Kirsten Foss Davis, Mark Fitz-Patrick, and Deborah J. Kiernan for providing logistical support.

Introduction

Martin Feldstein, James R. Hines, Jr.,
and R. Glenn Hubbard

This growing worldwide importance of international business activities has in recent years lead to serious reexaminations of the ways that governments tax multinational corporations. In the United States, much of the debate concerns the competitive positions of U.S. firms in international product and capital markets. In addition, there are those who argue that U.S. international tax rules have become more complex and more distorting in recent years, particularly since the passage of the Tax Reform Act of 1986. Discussions in the U.S. Congress and the administration since 1992 reveal a willingness to consider significant reforms. In Europe, increased liberalization of capital markets prompted the European Commission to discuss harmonization of corporate taxation. These policy developments not only suggest dissatisfaction with certain features of modern tax practice, but also raise deeper questions of whether current systems of taxing international income are viable in a world of significant capital market integration and global commercial competition.

Academic researchers have expressed renewed interest in studying the effects of taxation on capital formation and allocation, patterns of finance in multinational companies, international competition, and opportunities for income shifting and tax avoidance. This research brings together the approaches used by specialists in public finance and international economics. The papers presented in this volume summarize the results of a research program of the National Bureau of Economic Research on the effects of taxation on the invest-

Martin Feldstein is the George F. Baker Professor of Economics at Harvard University and president of the National Bureau of Economic Research. James R. Hines, Jr., is associate professor of public policy at the John F. Kennedy School of Government of Harvard University and a faculty research fellow of the National Bureau of Economic Research. R. Glenn Hubbard is the Russell L. Carson Professor of Economics and Finance at the Graduate School of Business of Columbia University and a research associate of the National Bureau of Economic Research.

ment and financing decisions of multinational corporations.[1] As a group, the papers describe the impact of U.S. firms' outbound foreign investment on the U.S. and foreign economies. The papers offer empirical evidence documenting channels through which tax policy in the United States and abroad affects plant and equipment investment, spending on R&D, the cost of debt and equity finance, and dividend repatriations by U.S. subsidiaries. The findings of these papers, described briefly below, will be useful in discussions of reforms of international tax rules in the United States and elsewhere. The current U.S. rules for taxing international income are summarized in an appendix at the end of the volume.

According to Robert Lipsey, overseas production contributes to the ability of American multinationals to retain world market shares in the face of a long-term decline in the U.S. share of world trade, and in the face of short-term changes (such as exchange rate fluctuations). Overseas production performs the same functions for Swedish firms and, more recently, for Japanese firms. Within U.S. multinationals, those with higher shares of production overseas have higher employment at home relative to production at home. Foreign production appears to require larger numbers of employees in headquarters activities (including R&D and supervision).

Martin Feldstein shows that the credit for foreign taxes paid does not induce U.S. firms to expand their foreign direct investment (FDI) enough so that the return on FDI to the United States is less than the return on the displaced domestic investment. Feldstein argues that a typical marginal investment overseas (which has the same net return to an American multinational parent as an alternative marginal domestic investment) actually generates a higher return for the United States than would the domestic investment it displaces. In order to maximize the present value of U.S. national income, one would not replace the current foreign tax credit with a deduction for foreign taxes. Instead, one would move in the opposite direction, encouraging more FDI in general, and investments that employ substantial foreign debt per dollar of U.S. capital in particular.

Joosung Jun modifies conventional cost-of-capital measures to incorporate the impact of international tax rules. He finds that corporate taxation of foreign investment causes U.S. firms operating in major foreign markets to face, on average, about 20 percent higher costs of capital than do domestic firms in the United States. Further, U.S. firms very likely face higher costs of capital than do local firms in foreign markets. U.S. firms operating in foreign markets also may have cost-of-capital disadvantages vis-à-vis firms from third countries, in part because the U.S. tax system is not integrated and in part because U.S. tax deferral and foreign tax credit calculation rules are so strict.

---

1. More-technical papers appear in the companion volume edited by Feldstein, Hines, and Hubbard (1995) and in earlier volumes edited by Razin and Slemrod (1990) and Giovannini, Hubbard, and Slemrod (1993).

Roger Gordon and Jeffrey MacKie-Mason examine possible explanations of why industrial countries tax the overseas income of their domestic multinational firms in the ways that they do. Many economists argue that it is inefficient to use corporate income taxes to raise revenue in open economies. If capital is internationally mobile, the burden of corporate taxes falls largely on other immobile factors (such as labor), and the tax system would be more efficient if these other factors were instead taxed directly. Not only do governments use corporate taxes, however, but corporate tax rates are also roughly comparable with top individual tax rates. Some theories predict that multinationals based in countries with residence-based tax systems should not invest in countries with low corporate tax rates, since those multinationals must pay sizable surtaxes when they repatriate their profits. This tax obligation imposes on these multinationals a competitive disadvantage, yet there is a significant amount of such FDI. Gordon and MacKie-Mason suggest that the abilities of firms to shift income (through aggressive transfer pricing) may explain the use of corporate income taxes, as well as the observed pattern of FDI. Countries may use corporate taxes as backstops to labor income taxes in order to discourage individuals from converting their labor incomes into otherwise-untaxed corporate income. The authors explore how those taxes might be modified to deal with cross-border income shifting.

Andrew Lyon and Gerald Silverstein examine some of the ways that U.S.-based multinational corporations may be affected by the corporate alternative minimum tax (AMT). In 1990, more than half of all the foreign-source income was earned by corporations subject to the AMT. Consequently, when U.S. firms plan their foreign activities, the tax incentives created by the AMT may be at least as important as those created by the regular U.S. corporate tax. The AMT creates a relative incentive for AMT firms to invest abroad rather than in the United States, and the AMT offers a temporary timing opportunity that allows repatriation of income from abroad at a lower cost than if the firm were subject to the rules of the regular U.S. tax system. These two different incentives have an ambiguous effect on U.S. domestic investment overall, if repatriated income is retained by the parent corporation in the United States. The AMT may provide an opportunity for firms to repatriate income from certain foreign locations with poor reinvestment opportunities, and at the same time to reinvest funds abroad in alternative foreign locations that have better investment opportunities. There appears to be an ambiguous net effect of these two incentives on the total volume of capital invested outside the United States.

James Hines asks first whether R&D activity by multinational firms is sensitive to local tax conditions, and second whether imported technology and R&D are complements or substitutes. He finds that R&D responds to local tax rates, and that it is a substitute for imported technology. Firms appear to react to high royalty tax rates by paying fewer royalties and performing additional R&D locally. To the extent that royalty payments reflect actual technology transfer (rather than adept accounting practices), the behavior of multinational firms suggests that local R&D is a substitute for imported technology.

Rosanne Altshuler, Scott Newlon, and William Randolph recognize that repatriation taxes on dividends may vary over time, providing firms with incentives to time repatriations so that they occur in years when repatriation tax rates are relatively low. The authors use information about cross-country differences in tax rates to distinguish the effects on dividend repatriations of permanent tax changes (as typically occur when statutory tax rates change) from the effects of transitory tax changes. Using data from U.S. tax returns for a large sample of U.S. corporations and their foreign subsidiaries, the authors find that permanent tax changes have much smaller effects than do the transitory tax changes. This finding suggests that repatriation taxes *do* affect dividend repatriation decisions, but only to the extent that taxes vary over time.

Jason Cummins and R. Glenn Hubbard use panel data on FDI by subsidiaries of U.S. multinational firms to measure the effect of taxation on FDI. The results cast significant doubt on the simplest notion that taxes do not influence U.S. firms' overseas investment decisions. Taxes appear to influence FDI in precisely the ways indicated by traditional neoclassical economic models of investment behavior. Specifically, it appears that the annual rate of overseas investment falls by 1–2 percentage points for each percentage point rise in the cost of capital for outbound FDI. This effect, which is of a magnitude similar to those recently estimated for domestic investment by U.S. and European firms, implies that changes in foreign corporate tax rates and depreciation rules, or in the foreign tax credit status of parent firms, significantly influence overseas investment by U.S. subsidiaries.

Kenneth Froot and James Hines examine the impact of the change in the U.S. interest allocation rules that followed passage of the Tax Reform Act of 1986. The 1986 act significantly limited the tax deductibility of the U.S. interest expenses of certain American multinational corporations. This tax change increased the tax liabilities of certain American multinationals and made additional borrowing more expensive for these firms. Froot and Hines find that the change in interest allocation rules discouraged borrowing and new investments. Firms that were unable to deduct all of their interest expenses against their U.S. tax liabilities issued 4.2 percent less debt (measured as a fraction of total firm assets) and invested 3.5 percent less in property, plant, and equipment during 1986–91 than other firms did. This is consistent with other evidence that suggests that the Tax Reform Act of 1986 significantly raised the borrowing costs of some American multinational firms.

Jason Cummins, Trevor Harris, and Kevin Hassett analyze the two accounting regimes that govern reporting practices in most developed countries. "One-book" countries, such as Germany, use their tax books as the basis for financial reporting. "Two-book" countries, including the United States, keep tax and financial reporting books largely separate. Firms in one-book countries may be reluctant to claim certain tax benefits if reductions in their taxable incomes can be misinterpreted by financial market participants as signals of lower profit-ability. The authors' estimates suggest that the interaction of tax systems and accounting regimes significantly influences domestic investment patterns, both within and across countries.

References

Feldstein, Martin, James R. Hines, Jr., and R. Glenn Hubbard, eds. 1995. *The effects of taxation on multinational corporations.* Chicago: University of Chicago Press.
Giovannini, Alberto, R. Glenn Hubbard, and Joel Slemrod, eds. 1993. *Studies in international taxation.* Chicago: University of Chicago Press.
Razin, Assaf, and Joel Slemrod, eds. 1990. *Taxation in the global economy.* Chicago: University of Chicago Press.

1   Home-Country Effects of Outward Direct Investment

Robert E. Lipsey

A decision to change the way American firms are taxed on the profits from their foreign operations must involve some judgment as to the desirability of increasing or decreasing the extent of U.S. firms' foreign operations. This paper reviews past research on the effects of the overseas operations of U.S. firms on the U.S. economy.

Four main topics are discussed here:

1. The growth and decline of U.S. firms' internationalized production
2. Overseas production and export market shares in manufacturing
3. Does foreign production substitute for home-country exports?
4. Foreign production and home-country labor

1.1   The Growth and Decline of U.S. Firms' Internationalized Production[1]

The establishment of foreign operations by American firms, and the establishment by any country's firms of production, including sales and service activities, outside the home country, is often referred to as the internationalization of production. The heyday of U.S. direct investment outflows, in the 1960s and at least part of the 1970s, involved considerable internationalization of U.S. firms' production, in the sense that higher and higher proportions of the production they controlled took place abroad, larger proportions of their employees were outside the United States, and larger shares of their assets came to be located abroad. Since then, however, the degree of internationalization of U.S. companies has stabilized or declined, as if the firms had overshot some desir-

Robert E. Lipsey is professor of economics at Queens College and the Graduate Center, City University of New York and a research associate of the National Bureau of Economic Research.
1. The data in this section are taken mainly from Lipsey 1993, 1994.

able level of foreign involvement and found it prudent to retreat somewhat. For example, employment in all overseas affiliates of U.S. firms was almost 11 percent of total U.S. nonagricultural employment in 1977, but only 7.5 percent in 1989.

U.S. manufacturing firms have long been much more internationalized than firms in other industries, with their overseas employment reaching about a quarter of domestic manufacturing employment in 1977 (from only 10 percent in 1957) and then declining slightly to about 22 percent in the late 1980s.

Within U.S. multinational manufacturing firms, the changes have not been so sharp. Foreign affiliate production was larger in the late 1980s relative to parent sales than in 1977, and affiliate employment was close to the earlier levels relative to parent employment. Thus, this group of firms has not exhibited the shift away from internationalized production that has characterized U.S. multinationals in general or the U.S. manufacturing sector as a whole.

The contrast between the changes in internationalization within U.S. firms and those in the U.S. economy as a whole reflects the declining role of multinational parents within the U.S. economy. Parent employment in the United States fell from 28 percent of U.S. nonagricultural employment in 1977 to barely over 20 percent in the late 1980s, not because employment was moved overseas, where affiliate employment was also declining, but because these multinationals were declining in importance as part of the U.S. economy. The shrinking of many large, established U.S. firms affected both their domestic and their foreign employment. The many anecdotes about the shifting of domestic employment abroad do not seem to add up to much in the aggregate, especially for the U.S. economy as a whole.

It is as yet difficult to judge whether the apparent retreat of U.S. firms from foreign operations during the 1980s is a long-term trend. There was an enormous shift in direct investment toward the United States by foreign firms, to the point where the United States absorbed an unprecedented share of the rest of the world's outflow of direct investment. Apparently, the United States was an exceptionally attractive location for investment during this period. If that was the case, it might also have been attractive, relative to locations in other countries, to American firms as well as to foreign firms. That attractiveness of the United States as a location would show up as a retreat from internationalization for U.S. firms while it tended to increase the degree of internationalization of foreign firms.

One reason for American firms' apparent retreat from overseas activity may have been the growth of efficient and aggressive foreign competitors. The levels of internationalization of the German and Japanese economies were much lower than that of the United States in the 1970s. Since then, the internationalization pioneered on a large scale by American firms has been copied by European and Japanese firms.

The practice of producing outside the home country is well entrenched, especially in manufacturing. Increasingly, it is the practice not only for firms based in the major industrial countries, but also for firms in at least the more successful developing countries, such as Korea and Taiwan.

1.2   Overseas Production and Export Market Shares in Manufacturing[2]

The share of the United States, as a country, in world export markets for manufactured goods has been declining over most of the last quarter century. In 1991 and 1992, the share was about 12.5 percent, more than 25 percent below the share in 1966. U.S. multinational manufacturing firms, exporting both from the United States and from their overseas production, held on to their shares much more successfully. By 1985, when the United States had already lost more than 20 percent of its share of twenty years earlier, U.S. multinationals had increased their share of world manufactured exports. By 1991, their share was only 4 percent below that of 1966.

How was this relative stability of shares achieved? A rising percentage of the multinationals' exports was supplied by their overseas affiliates: more than half since 1986. Thus, one way the U.S. multinationals kept their export markets, as the United States lost competitiveness in their industries, was by supplying these markets increasingly from overseas operations, a strategy obviously not available to nonmultinational U.S. firms.

The United States, Japan, and Sweden are the only countries that collect fairly comprehensive information on the trade of their multinationals' overseas affiliates. The data for all three countries suggest that one major role for overseas production by firms in all three countries has been retaining market shares when home-country economic conditions and exchange rate changes made the home countries less suitable locations for export production.

1.3   Does Foreign Production Substitute for Home-Country Exports?[3]

Most antagonism against foreign direct investment has historically been toward inward investment, on the ground that it displaced home-country firms in home markets. There has also been opposition to outward investment, however, often led by labor organizations, on the ground that outward investment "exports jobs," partly by producing products to be imported to the home-country market but mostly by replacing home-country exports by overseas affiliates' production.

Various studies (including some of my own) of the behavior of multinational firms view them as facing fixed or relatively fixed, worldwide markets for their products and making decisions mainly about how to supply that demand most profitably. The firm is pictured as choosing to supply the demand by exporting from the home country, by producing abroad, or by licensing technology,

2. For a more detailed discussion, see Lipsey 1994.
3. For a more detailed discussion and references, see Lipsey 1994.

patents, or other assets owned by the firm to foreign licensees who would produce outside the home country.

The assumption of a fixed market for a firm tends to bias the results toward finding that foreign production by a country's firms substitutes for home production. A more plausible view, I think, is that production abroad is often mainly a way of enlarging a firm's share of foreign markets, or of preventing or slowing a decline in that share. The inadequacy of the fixed-market assumption is obvious in any attempt to examine the impact of direct investment in service industries, since the nature of many of these industries precludes substantial exporting from one country to another and market share is almost completely contingent on production at the site of consumption. While this is most obvious for service industries, it applies also to the service component of manufacturing industries, a major part of the final value of sales of manufactured products.

Attempts to answer the question of the effect of overseas production on home-country exports face the problem of defining substitution and of constructing a believable counterfactual case. Exports from Japan's recently established or recently enlarged operations in Southeast Asia may replace exports that formerly came from Japan, but few would claim, after the rise in the exchange value of the yen, that they are replacing exports that could now be made from Japan.

There have been quite a few empirical studies of the impact of overseas production on home-country exports, based on both U.S. and Swedish data. The preponderance of evidence from these studies points to either no effect or a positive effect of overseas production in a host-country market on home-country exports to that market and of production by a firm's foreign affiliates in a market on the parent firm's exports to that market.

On the whole, then, it would seem reasonable to conclude that production outside the United States by U.S.-shared firms has little effect on exports from the United States by parent firms or by all U.S. firms as a whole. To the extent that there is an effect, it is more likely to be positive than negative. This relationship is probably a characteristic of other countries' multinationals as well. One reason this is true is that foreign production is undertaken to expand or to retain a parent firm's foreign markets. There is no indication that the absolute level of imports from the home country declines over long periods.

1.4 Foreign Production and Home-Country Labor[4]

Since overseas production does not appear to have any substantial impact on the amount of parent exports, one could assume that parent production levels are not substantially affected. However, overseas production could affect the overall demand for labor within the United States by parent firms, and the demand for labor of different types, even if total production in the United States were not affected. For example, the demand for labor by parent firms might be reduced if more labor-intensive products were allocated to multi-

4. For further discussion and references, see Kravis and Lipsey 1988, 1992a; Lipsey 1994.

nationals' foreign operations while more capital-intensive operations were allocated to U.S. operations. Similarly, the demand for unskilled labor by parents might decline if parts of the production process or products requiring highly skilled labor were allocated to the United States while processes or products requiring relatively low skills were allocated to overseas affiliates.

The opportunity for multinational firms to engage in such geographical allocation of their production presumably requires that the product be tradable. If a firm's output must be consumed where it is produced, as in many service industries, production will take place where the goods and services are sold and will respond to host-country demand and to host-country costs.

On the whole, the evidence suggests that in both manufacturing and service industries the effect of foreign operations on the average skill levels in parent companies was to raise them, but the effect was not strong and not universal across industries.

1.5   Summary

The explanation of the existence of direct investment and foreign production is centered on the idea that firms possess individual firm-specific assets, such as technologies, patents, and skills in advertising or marketing, that can be exploited most profitably by producing in many markets. These assets are mobile across international borders but not among firms, and firms cannot realize their value by selling them to other firms or by renting them to other firms by licensing.

The opportunity to exploit these firm-specific assets via direct investment adds to the incentive to acquire them. If R&D intensity and human-capital intensity are the strongest explanations of the worldwide trade shares of U.S. multinationals (Kravis and Lipsey 1992b), and possibly of their shares in world production as well, a restriction on direct investment would reduce the value of investment in such assets and therefore reduce firms' investment in them. If much of foreign direct investment is defensive, as suggested earlier, it may make investment in firm-specific assets more profitable by extending the length of time over which they can be exploited, a suggestion made many years ago by Vernon (1966).

While firms from different countries tend to possess different comparative advantages, the leading firms in each country tend to internationalize their production. With the long-term decline in costs of international travel and communication, the costs of controlling widespread production must be declining, and firms from most countries are increasing the extent to which they produce outside their home countries. With that fact as background, it seems unlikely that the decline in internationalization of American firms' production will go much further, and more likely that it will be reversed.

The availability of foreign production locations appears to have contributed a great deal to the ability of American multinational firms to retain their market shares in the face of declines in the market share of the United States as a country. The same seems to be true for the trade shares of firms from other countries, and this flexibility applies to softening the effects not only of long-term national declines but also of short-term events such as large changes in exchange rates.

The frequently expressed fear that American multinationals have been, in some sense, "exporting jobs" by substituting foreign production for American production has very little empirical support. For one thing, overseas employment and fixed investment have been for the most part declining relative to domestic employment and fixed investment for ten or fifteen years. And U.S. firms that produce more abroad than others tend also to export more in general and to the countries where the foreign production takes place. The same relationship is evident for firms based in Sweden, the only other country collecting similar data on multinational parents and affiliates. Overseas production has much more to do with contesting market shares than with finding low-cost production locations, although the latter is also a motivation.

Within multinational firms, the higher the share of overseas operations in the total production of the multinational, the higher the ratio of home employment to home production, more often than not. A possible explanation is that a larger share of foreign production requires a larger number of headquarters employees, such as R&D staff and supervisory personnel, whose contribution to output is not confined to the firm's domestic production.

On the whole, the evidence suggests that the effect of overseas production on the home-country labor market involves the composition of a firm's employment at home rather than the total amount of its home employment. That shift in employment composition is mainly toward more managerial and technical employment.

References

Kravis, Irving B., and Robert E. Lipsey. 1988. The Effect of Multinational Firms' Foreign Operations on Their Domestic Employment. NBER Working Paper no. 2760. Cambridge, MA: National Bureau of Economic Research, November.

———. 1992a. Parent Firms and Their Foreign Subsidiaries in Goods and Service Industries. In International Trade and Finance Association: 1992 Proceedings, ed. Khosrow Fatemi, 207–22. Laredo, TX: International Trade and Finance Association.

———. 1992b. Sources of Competitiveness of the United States and of Its Multinational Firms. Review of Economics and Statistics 74 (2): 193–201.

Lipsey, Robert E. 1993. The Transnationalization of Economic Activity. Paper prepared for the Programme on Transnational Corporations, United Nations Conference on Trade and Development, Geneva.

———. 1994. Outward Direct Investment and the U.S. Economy. NBER Working Paper no. 4691. Cambridge, MA: National Bureau of Economic Research, March.

Vernon, Raymond. 1966. International Investment and International Trade in the Product Cycle. Quarterly Journal of Economics 80 (May): 190–207.

2   Tax Rules and the Effect of Foreign Direct Investment on U.S. National Income

Martin Feldstein

2.1 Introduction

Do existing tax rules cause the volume of outbound foreign direct investment (FDI) from the United States to be excessive in the sense that a decrease in the current level of such investments would raise the present value of U.S. national income? The evidence discussed in this paper suggests the opposite is true. The present value of the repatriated dividends and interest that would result from an additional dollar of outbound FDI would exceed the present value of the income that would result from a one dollar increase in domestic investment in business plant and equipment.[1] Thus, even if each dollar of outbound FDI displaces a dollar of domestic investment, an incremental expansion of outbound FDI would raise the present value of U.S. national income.

It is, of course, widely recognized that much of U.S. outbound FDI allows parent firms to earn especially high rates of return based on their existing patents, technical know-how, brand names, and other assets that cannot be fully exploited by producing at home and exporting or by licensing to foreign firms. The relevant economic question is therefore not about the desirability of outbound FDI as a whole, but about the appropriate extent of such investment. Critics argue that the existing U.S. tax rules induce firms to increase their overseas direct investment to a point at which the national return to the United

Martin Feldstein is the George F. Baker Professor of Economics at Harvard University and president of the National Bureau of Economic Research.

The author is grateful to Jim Hines for discussions about these issues, to Joosung Jun for advice about data sources and measurement issues, and to Todd Sinai for help with the regression analysis summarized in section 2.3.

1. The present analysis integrates research presented in Feldstein (1994).

States on that investment is less than the national return on an additional dollar of domestic investment.[2]

The analysis that leads to that conclusion can be summarized as follows:[3] U.S. parent firms receive a tax credit in the United States for the taxes paid by foreign subsidiaries to foreign governments (up to the tax rate that would be paid to the U.S. government on those profits). Since the parent firm is indifferent between paying taxes to foreign governments and to the U.S. government, the parent expands foreign subsidiary investment to the point at which the after-tax return to the firm is the same abroad and at home. Because the after-tax return abroad is the total return to the United States while the pretax return on domestic investment is the total return to the United States, the U.S. national return on the last dollar of outbound FDI is less than the national return on the last dollar of domestic investment. Equating the national returns on both types of investment requires replacing the credit for foreign taxes with a deduction (which treats foreign taxes paid like any other business expense).[4]

This widely accepted argument is wrong because it ignores the combined impact of debt finance and the imperfect integration of the world capital market. The evidence summarized below indicates that the FDI of U.S. multinational firms causes those firms to borrow more from foreign sources than they otherwise would. Because the after-tax cost of that capital is less than the after-tax return on the investments made abroad, the parent firm gains a net advantage. Unlike domestic borrowing in the United States (which just shifts the income among the providers of debt and equity capital and the government), this foreign borrowing represents a transfer from the fixed income investors (lenders) in the foreign country to the United States. With the actual prevailing patterns of finance and tax rates, the net advantage of foreign borrowing exceeds the disadvantage of paying taxes to the foreign government. The estimates described below indicate that FDI at the margin leads to a stream of net interest and dividend receipts to the United States with a present value of more than $1.72 for every dollar of outbound direct investment.[5]

Although this net advantage could in principle be achieved by international

2. This argument is quite separate from the popular debate about whether outbound FDI reduces employment in the United States because it substitutes for domestic production and exporting or increases employment in the United States because parent firms export to their foreign subsidiaries. Economists recognize that this is a misplaced concern because the American labor market works well in assuring that all who want jobs at wages that reflect their skills can find work within a relatively short time. See Graham and Krugman 1991 and Lipsey 1995.

3. This argument, first presented in Richman 1963 and Musgrave 1969 and later formalized in Dutton 1982, has been widely accepted in tax-policy discussions (e.g., U.S. Congress, Joint Committee on Taxation 1991).

4. The use of a foreign tax credit is sometimes justified as a way of maximizing the global return to capital, that is, inducing firms to expand outbound FDI until the pretax return is the same in all countries. Horst (1980) shows that this issue is more complicated when the saving rate reflects the after-tax return on investment.

5. This present value is calculated at 12 percent, the real rate of return assumed to be earned (pretax) on incremental U.S. domestic investments in business capital.

portfolio investment without any FDI, the very imperfect integration of the world capital market means that this does not happen in practice. Section 2.2 discusses the nature of the imperfect global capital market integration and the way in which FDI circumvents the limited net movement of portfolio capital. Section 2.3 deals more explicitly with the effect of FDI on the level of domestic investment, and section 2.4 discusses the effect of such investment on the use of foreign debt and equity capital by American multinational corporations. The implications of this for the present value of the dividend and interest payments that are generated by outbound FDI are presented in section 2.5. There is a very brief concluding section.

2.2   The Limited Integration of World Capital Markets and the Circumventing Effect of FDI

If the national capital markets around the globe were fully integrated into a single global capital market, a dollar of additional saving in any country would flow to the investment anywhere in the world that offered the highest rate of return, regardless of national boundaries. There is, however, strong and robust evidence that this does not happen. Despite the large volume of gross international capital flows, there is very little net capital flow. Saving generated in any country tends to stay in that country.

The evidence on this "home bias" in international capital markets indicates that a sustained increase in the ratio of domestic savings to gross domestic product (GDP) causes a sustained increase in domestic investment that is approximately 80 percent to 90 percent as large. This 80 percent to 90 percent "saving retention ratio" has been confirmed many times since it was first presented by Feldstein and Horioka (1980) and has been shown to be robust with respect to the time period, the estimation method, and the subsample of countries.[6] This conclusion, based on cross-country studies of decade average saving and investment rates, is consistent with detailed microeconomic evidence showing that only a very small fraction of the portfolios of large institutions are invested abroad. Moreover, only about 3 percent of the total U.S. private financial wealth of $9.4 trillion at the end of 1991 was invested in foreign stocks and bonds.

This segmentation of the global capital market implies that an international flow of portfolio funds or bank loans does not automatically equalize the return on investments in different countries or the cost of funds to borrowers in different countries. It also has important implications for the impact of FDI. In a perfectly integrated world capital market, an incremental dollar of capital outflow from the United States in the form of FDI might be offset by a net inflow

---

6. See, for example, the papers by Feldstein and Bacchetta (1991) and Frankel (1985, 1991). Mussa and Goldstein (1993) present an excellent summary and interpretation of this literature.

of an additional dollar of portfolio capital, leaving domestic investment unchanged. The evidence summarized in the next section indicates that this does not happen in practice. An increase in outbound FDI appears to increase the outflow of domestic saving to the rest of the world.

A second way that FDI circumvents the segmentation of global capital markets is through the local financing of the foreign subsidiary. The evidence summarized in section 2.4 shows that the subsidiaries of U.S. multinational companies use substantially more foreign-source debt than domestic U.S. companies do. Although this does not cause a cross-border flow of capital, it does give U.S. equity investors an opportunity to use more foreign debt capital than they would without the outbound FDI. The importance of this for the national return on outbound FDI is discussed in section 2.5.

2.3 The Effect of Outbound FDI on Domestic Investment

To understand the likely effect of outbound FDI on the aggregate volume of domestic investment, it is useful to begin with an analysis of the behavior of an individual multinational firm and then to consider the broader general equilibrium response of the capital market to the action of the firm.

A simplified version of corporate capital budgeting shows how a firm's decision to invest abroad could cause an equal reduction in its domestic investment. The company starts with a given projected level of after-tax profits for the current year. The management pays a current dividend based on the past level of dividends and shareholders' expectations about the link between dividends and reported earnings. The amount of retained earnings that remains after that dividend and the company's desired ratio of debt to capital together determine the amount that the company can borrow during the current year and therefore the firm's total funds available for capital investments. The company could supplement these funds by new equity issues or divestitures or could absorb some of these funds by share repurchases, but such transactions are unusual events rather than a part of the annual capital budgeting process. This capital budgeting process is carried out at the level of the corporation as a whole and not for the parent company or for any of the subsidiaries alone. Any portion of the total capital budget that is used for one investment reduces the funds available for other investments. In particular, an increase in the total amount of overseas investment reduces the amount of capital available for domestic investment within the firm by an equal amount.

Such a reduction in domestic investment within a single firm that makes an overseas direct investment does not imply anything about the effect of aggregate outbound FDI on the aggregate level of domestic investment within the U.S. economy as a whole. For example, the domestic investment opportunity that the firm forgoes because it invests abroad might be undertaken by another firm that would otherwise have invested those funds abroad. But when the entire business sector is aggregated, it is clear that a net increase in aggregate

FDI will reduce domestic investment by an equal amount if all firms use the type of capital budgeting process described above.

It is possible, however, that this description of the capital budgeting process is too restrictive. A sustained rise in total national outbound FDI could in principle leave domestic investment opportunities that induce firms to raise their debt-to-capital ratio with the additional funds coming from abroad. In other words, the increase in outbound FDI would induce an offsetting inflow of portfolio capital. The effect of outbound FDI on total domestic investment thus depends on the extent to which portfolio capital is internationally mobile.

To assess this, I have extended the earlier Feldstein-Horioka (1980) analysis of investment in the major industrial countries of the Organization for Economic Cooperation and Development. To do so, I have estimated regression equations with decade average ratios of gross domestic investment to GDP as the dependent variable and with the gross national saving ratio (GNS/GDP) and the FDI ratios (FDI-out/GDP and FDI-in/GDP) as the key explanatory variables. Other control variables that are likely to influence the investment rate and to be correlated with the FDI-out/GDP ratio are also included in the equation: the absolute size of the economy, an indication of whether it is a European country, the rate of real economic growth, the rate of inflation, and the rate of interest. The estimated coefficient of the ratio of FDI-out to GDP in such an equation is about -1 (varying between -0.80 and -1.59 according to the decade of the data and the specific control variables included) and with large enough standard errors that in every case it is not significantly different from -1.[7] This indicates that each dollar of outbound FDI displaces approximately one dollar of domestic investment, a result that is consistent with the view that the Feldstein-Horioka capital market segmentation applies to portfolio capital and that FDI achieves a net cross-border flow of capital equal to the amount of the FDI.

2.4   The Effect of Outbound FDI on the Use of Foreign Capital

The cross-border capital flow that was discussed in the previous section represents only a small part of the total financing of the foreign affiliates of U.S. multinationals. The Commerce Department's *U.S. Direct Investment Abroad: 1989 Benchmark Survey* (1992) found that among majority-owned nonbank affiliates of U.S. nonbank companies only about 20 percent of the value of assets owned abroad is financed by cross-border flows from the United States. An additional 18 percent represents retained earnings attributable to U.S. parents. The remaining 62 percent is financed locally by foreign debt and equity, of which foreign debt is about 53 percent and foreign equity is the remaining 9 percent.[8]

---

7. The specific estimates are presented in table 2.3 of Feldstein 1995.
8. More details on this capital are presented in section 1 of Feldstein 1994.

This use of foreign capital is far greater than it would be for additional domestic investments, perhaps reflecting a greater willingness of foreign banks and other lenders to provide credit to local subsidiaries of U.S. firms that have local assets as implicit collateral. In addition, the parent firm may use foreign debt to hedge the effect of currency fluctuations on the value of reported overseas earnings. The multinational parent may also use local borrowing as a way to reduce expropriation risk. Whatever the reason, it is clear that U.S. firms borrow much more foreign funds when they have direct investments abroad. In this way, the flow of FDI also overcomes the apparent segmentation of the global capital market.

2.5   The Present Value of Dividends and Interest per Dollar of FDI

The preceding analysis indicates the information needed to assess the impact on the United States of an incremental dollar of U.S. outbound FDI. Consider a firm for which the real pretax rate of return on an incremental investment in the United States would be 12 percent. If the tax rate faced by the firm's foreign affiliate is the same as the U.S. tax rate and the leverage used abroad is the same as the leverage at home, the firm will invest until the marginal pretax return on the foreign investment is also 12 percent.

From the point of view of the United States as a whole, there are two fundamental differences between the firm's domestic and foreign investment. First, the foreign investment will be taxed by the government of the foreign country, so that the entire 12 percent pretax return does not flow to the United States. In contrast, the tax collected on the firm's investment in the United States remains U.S. national income. Second, the borrowing by the foreign affiliate at an after-tax cost that is substantially less than the real return on capital confers a net benefit to the United States. In contrast, when the firm borrows domestically to finance the alternative domestic investment, the gap between the return on capital and the net cost of borrowing is simply a redistribution among equity owners, lenders, and the government with no net impact on U.S. national income.

The net impact of these two countervailing forces can be evaluated by estimating the present value of the dividends and interest (net of future lending from the United States) that would be paid to U.S. suppliers of capital on the incremental foreign investment. The present value of U.S. national income is increased by the incremental FDI if the present value of these flows, when discounted at the 12 percent real rate of return that would have been earned on the displaced U.S. investment, exceeds the initial value of the displaced investment.

In Feldstein (1994) I estimate this stream of dividends and interest (net of future lending from the United States) for a foreign investment with a financing pattern that corresponds to the mix of U.S.- and foreign-source debt and equity described in section 2.4 above. More specifically, each dollar of initial assets abroad is financed with a mix of U.S. and foreign equity and debt. The U.S. investors provide 70 percent of the equity and 8 percent of the debt, essentially the ratios implied by the *U.S. Direct Investment Abroad: 1989 Benchmark Survey.* The debt finance equals 50 percent of the total capital investment. Annual dividends are equal to 70 percent of after-tax profits. The remaining retained earnings are leveraged with an equal amount of debt, with 8 percent of that incremental debt coming from U.S. sources and 92 percent coming from foreign sources. The interest rate is 8 percent, and inflation is 4 percent.

The present value of the net interest and dividends paid to U.S. investors that are generated by this process is $1.72 per dollar of initial U.S. debt and equity investment when discounted at a 12 percent real discount rate.[9] Even with the conservative assumption that each dollar of cross-border FDI displaces a full dollar of domestic investment and that all of that investment would have earned the 12 percent available on additions to the business capital stock (rather than the lower return available on owner-occupied housing), this calculation implies that each dollar of outbound FDI raises the present value of U.S. national income by nearly twice as much as the value of the displaced investment. Measured in a different way, the assumptions described in the previous paragraph imply that the U.S. cross-border investment earns an internal rate of return for the United States of 15.1 percent.

2.6   Concluding Remarks

It is clear from the analysis in this paper that the credit for foreign taxes paid does not induce U.S. firms to expand FDI to a point at which the return to the United States on such investments is less than the return on the displaced domestic investment. A typical marginal FDI (which has the same net return to an American multinational parent as an alternative marginal domestic investment) actually has a higher return to the United States than the domestic investment that it displaces.

A rule for taxing FDI to maximize the present value of U.S. national income would certainly not replace the current foreign tax credit with a deduction for foreign taxes. It would instead move in the opposite direction from the current tax rule in order to encourage more FDI, particularly investments that employ substantial foreign debt per dollar of U.S. capital.

---

9. The net flow to the United States is the interest and dividends received minus the additional lending from U.S. sources. The analysis assumes that the incremental lending from U.S. sources continues to be 8 percent of the affiliate's total debt.

References

Dutton, John. 1982. The Optimal Taxation of International Investment Income: A Comment. *Quarterly Journal of Economics* 97 (May): 373–80.

Feldstein, Martin. 1994. Taxes, Leverage and the National Return on Outbound Foreign Direct Investment. NBER Working Paper no. 4689. Cambridge, MA: National Bureau of Economic Research, March.

Feldstein, Martin. 1995. The Effects of Outbound Foreign Investment on the Domestic Capital Stock. In *The Effects of Taxation on Multinational Corporations,* ed. Martin Feldstein, James R. Hines, Jr., and R. Glenn Hubbard. Chicago: University of Chicago Press.

Feldstein, Martin, and P. Bacchetta. 1991. National Saving and International Investment. In *National Saving and Economic Performance,* ed. B. D. Bernheim and J. B. Shoven. Chicago: University of Chicago Press.

Feldstein, Martin, and Charles Horioka. 1980. Domestic Saving and International Capital Flows. *Economic Journal* 90 (June): 314–29.

Frankel, Jeffrey. 1985. International Capital Mobility and Crowding Out in the U.S. Economy. In *How Open Is the U.S. Economy,* ed. R. Hafer. Lexington, MA: Lexington Books.

———. 1991. Quantifying International Capital Mobility in the 1980s. In *National Saving and Economic Performance,* ed. B. D. Bernheim and J. B. Shoven. Chicago: University of Chicago Press.

Graham, Edward, and Paul Krugman. 1991. *Foreign Direct Investment in the United States.* Washington, DC: Institute for International Economics.

Horst, Thomas. 1980. A Note on Optimal Taxation of International Investment Income. *Quarterly Journal of Economics* 94 (June): 793–99.

Lipsey, Robert, 1995. Outward Direct Investment and the U.S. Economy. In *The Effects of Taxation on Multinational Corporations,* ed. Martin Feldstein, James R. Hines, Jr., and R. Glenn Hubbard. Chicago: University of Chicago Press.

Musgrave, Peggy B. 1969. *United States Taxation of Foreign Investment Income: Issues and Arguments.* Cambridge: Law School of Harvard University.

Mussa, Michael, and Morris Goldstein. 1993. The Integration of World Capital Markets. In *Changing Capital Markets: Implications for Monetary Policy.* 1993 Annual Conference of the Kansas City Federal Reserve Bank. Kansas City, MO: Kansas City Federal Reserve Bank.

Richman, Peggy B. 1963. *Taxation of Foreign Investment Income: An Economic Analysis.* Baltimore: Johns Hopkins University Press.

U.S. Congress. Joint Committee on Taxation. 1991. *Factors Affecting the International Competitiveness of the United States.* Washington, DC: Government Printing Office.

U.S. Department of Commerce. 1992. *U.S. Direct Investment Abroad: 1989 Benchmark Survey, Final Results.* Washington, DC: Government Printing Office.

3 Corporate Taxes and the Cost of Capital for U.S. Multinationals

Joosung Jun

3.1 Introduction

Tax rules affect the ability of U.S. firms to compete in foreign markets with local and other foreign firms. The primary channel through which taxes exert this influence is by changing the cost of capital. The competitive ability of firms that face different costs of capital depends on how capital intensive they are and how sensitive the demand for their product is to the price. This paper does not attempt to look at specific products, but does estimate how tax rules alter the cost of capital for U.S. firms and competing firms in a variety of foreign markets.

Past comparative studies of the cost of capital have been mostly concerned with domestic investment between countries. A typical finding of these studies is that, during the past decade, the cost-of-capital gap between countries has been largely attributable to differences in the domestic cost of funds, leaving relatively little room for the role of tax systems.

In the case of multinational investment, however, an international comparison of the cost of capital is complicated by the possibility of overlapping tax jurisdictions and the possibility of raising investment funds in different countries and transferring those funds between the parent and the subsidiary. Thus, comparing the cost of capital for domestic investment between countries may lead to very misleading implications for the competitiveness of multinationals.

This paper attempts to modify the conventional cost-of-capital measure in a way that incorporates the impact of international tax rules. The analysis compares measures of the cost of capital for U.S. firms and their local competitors in major foreign markets, and those of U.S. firms and other foreign multi-

Joosung Jun is assistant professor of economics at Ewha University.

nationals in a given foreign market. The evidence presented in this paper suggests that, other things being equal, corporate tax rules related to foreign investment make U.S. firms operating in major foreign markets, on average, face about a 20 percent higher cost of capital than domestic firms in the United States when U.S. source equity capital is considered as the marginal source of investment funds. These U.S. firms may very likely face a higher cost of equity capital than local firms in foreign markets. U.S. firms may also face a cost-of-capital disadvantage vis-à-vis firms from other countries in a given foreign market, partly due to the absence of a dividend imputation scheme in the United States and partly due to relatively strict U.S. rules regarding the exemption or deferral of home-country tax on foreign-source income and foreign tax credit utilization.

3.2   The Cost of Capital for Foreign Investment

The appendix to this volume describes the features of tax systems that apply to multinational corporations. This section sets out a framework within which the cost of capital for foreign investment is estimated. The focus is on the way in which corporate tax rules related to international investment influence the cost of capital.

All shareholders are assumed to live and be taxed in the home country. The foreign subsidiary is wholly owned by the domestic parent, which maximizes shareholder wealth. While the subsidiary can finance its investment through a variety of sources, this paper focuses on the case where the parent uses its retained earnings as the basic source of funds for both domestic and foreign investment in order to highlight the differential tax effects on domestic and foreign investment, given the same cost of funds. This paper also ignores personal taxes and focuses on the role of corporate taxes in determining the cost of capital.

The cost of capital is the pretax rate of return that a corporation must earn in order to pay the rate of return required by the providers of capital. The cost of capital depends on the discount rate as well as several other considerations such as the tax treatment of capital income and the depreciation of the investment asset.

The discount rate for domestic investment is determined by the rate of return required by the shareholders, which is the risk-adjusted rate of return on alternative investment opportunities. What is the appropriate discount rate for financing foreign investment? Taking the parent to be a conduit between foreign investment and the shareholders, the discount rate for foreign investment should reflect the taxes associated with repatriated dividends. Let u be the total tax rate on repatriated foreign-source dividends. The parent, whose objective is to maximize the wealth of its shareholders, then requires that foreign investment earn a yield of at least $1/(1 - u)$ dollars per dollar of transfers. Therefore, the required rate of return on foreign investment is larger than that for domestic investment by the factor of $1/(1 - u)$.

The effective tax rate on foreign-source dividends (u) consists of both host-country and home-country components, as described fully in Jun 1995. Suppose, for example, that domestic and foreign corporate tax rates and the withholding tax rate are 0.5, 0.4, and 0.05, respectively. Under the exemption system, the discount rate for foreign investment will be 5 percent larger than that for domestic investment using the same source of funds. Under the credit system, however, the home country taxes at the rate of 17 cents per dollar of dividends paid by the subsidiary. This surtax translates into a 20 percent higher discount rate.

In the remainder of the paper, various cost-of-capital measures for U.S. firms and their major competitors in foreign markets are presented. The methodology used to calculate the cost of capital is fully described in Jun 1995. A common real interest rate of 5 percent and a common inflation rate of 4.5 percent were assumed for the purposes of focusing on how the tax codes affect the cost of capital and of maintaining comparability between countries.

In summary, the cost-of-capital measures reported in the following sections are the pretax rates of return necessary to earn a given after-corporate-tax rate of return (real interest rate) of 5 percent. All the variations in the cost of capital for foreign investment across countries are purely due to differences in their corporate tax systems. The values for tax parameters are drawn from Organization for Economic Cooperation and Development 1991, and relate to the systems in force as of 1 January 1991.

3.3   U.S. versus Local Firms in Foreign Markets

Consider first the cost of capital for U.S. firms and their local competitors in major foreign markets in table 3.1. The first column reports the cost of capital for domestic investment. The effects of corporate tax rules on the cost of capital differentials for domestic investment between countries do not appear to be large, which is in line with most previous comparative studies. Across countries, the required pretax rates of return on domestic investment are higher in Japan, Germany, Italy, and Australia than in other countries, reflecting their relatively high corporate tax rates.

Now consider the case of U.S. firms investing in foreign markets (column 2). In the sample host countries, U.S. firms face about a 20 percent higher cost of equity capital on average than in the case of U.S. domestic investment (9.3 percent versus 7.6 percent). A 20 percent higher cost of capital for foreign investment might put U.S. multinationals in a disadvantageous position in most foreign markets. Comparing the two columns indicates that U.S. firms face a higher cost of equity capital than their local counterparts in every sample country other than Germany.

Table 3.1   The Cost of Capital for U.S. and Local Firms in Foreign Markets

Host Country	Local Firms	U.S. Firms
United States domestic	7.6	7.6
Japan	9.0	10.6
Canada	8.1	9.5
France	7.3	9.7
Germany	9.5	8.3
Netherlands	7.1	7.8
United Kingdom	7.7	8.6
Italy	9.1	9.9
Sweden	7.2	8.8
Switzerland	6.6	8.2
Australia	9.0	11.5
Average (foreign investment)	8.0	9.3

When only corporate taxes are considered, for example, U.S. domestic firms face a slightly lower cost of capital (7.6 percent) than do Japanese domestic firms (9.0 percent) because of higher corporate tax rates in Japan. Because of the tax costs associated with international investment, U.S. multinational firms face a higher cost of equity capital than do local firms in Japan (10.6 percent versus 9.0 percent), according to the calculations that underlie the figures reported in table 3.1. It has been noted in the literature that Japanese firms have enjoyed a cost-of-capital advantage over U.S. firms due mainly to the difference in the cost of funds between the two countries during the past decade. Since the results reported in this study are based on the assumption that there are no cost-of-funds differentials between countries, the negative impact of international tax rules on the cost of capital can be interpreted as an additional source of disadvantage for U.S. firms operating in Japan when these firms draw transfers from their domestic parents.

3.4   U.S. versus Other Multinationals in Foreign Markets

In a foreign market, U.S. firms compete not only with local firms but also with multinationals from other countries. Table 3.2 shows the cost-of-capital measures for firms from different countries operating in Japan.

In column 1, the cost of capital for U.S. firms is in the lower end of the spectrum (10.6 percent). Note that those firms whose cost of capital is higher than U.S. firms' are from countries with a dividend credit scheme (Canada, France, Germany, the Netherlands, the United Kingdom, Italy, and Australia). In these countries, the cost of two sources of parent equity funds—new equity and retained earnings—may be different. Since personal taxes (therefore, a personal tax advantage for capital gains relative to dividends) are ignored in this paper, the dividend imputation scheme will make the cost of parent new

Table 3.2   The Cost of Capital for Firms Operating in Japan

Home Country	Equity Transfers with No Imputation Credits for Foreign-Source Dividends	Equity Transfers with Imputation Credits for Foreign-Source Dividends
Japanese domestic	9.0	9.0
United States	10.6	10.6
Canada	11.1	7.3
France	11.7	6.8
Germany	12.8	2.4
Netherlands	10.6	10.6
United Kingdom	11.3	6.4
Italy	11.8	4.6
Sweden	10.6	10.6
Switzerland	10.6	10.6
Australia	13.9	4.7
Average (foreign investment)	11.5	7.5

equity lower than that for parent retained earnings for financing domestic investment.

If shareholders in these countries are allowed to take such dividend-imputation credits for foreign-source dividends, multinationals from these countries can lower the cost of capital for foreign investment by using parent new equity instead of parent retained earnings as the source of transfers. In this case, as shown in table 3.2, firms from countries with a dividend-imputation scheme have a clear advantage over U.S. firms. For example, the average cost of capital for firms from imputation countries is 5.4 percent, which is about half the cost of capital for U.S. firms. This result suggests the potential importance of integrating personal and corporate taxation in enhancing U.S. competitiveness.

Some countries try to restrict investors' ability to use the dividend-imputation scheme on dividends from domestic corporations financed by earnings from abroad. Typically, countries require that dividends eligible for the dividend-imputation scheme be less than the firm's after-tax profits from domestic operations. Unless a firm desires an abnormally high dividend payout rate, however, this restriction is unlikely to be binding.

There are several additional factors that may add to the competitive burden of U.S. firms operating abroad. Among major international investor countries, the United States has the tightest rules regarding the extent to which home-country taxes on foreign-source income are exempted or deferred and regarding the limitation of foreign tax credits. For example, the Tax Reform Act of 1986 has made pooling of worldwide income more difficult for U.S. firms by confining the eligibility to earnings from majority-owned subsidiaries while many other countries tried to adopt the exemption method by statutes or by treaties; unlike its major competitors, the United States considers loans a subsidiary makes to its parent to be the equivalent of a dividend to which a U.S. surtax may be applied; a recent U.S. tax bill (H.R. 5270, the Foreign Income Tax Rationalization and Simplification Act of 1992) includes a provision that repeals tax deferral; the United States is the only major developed country that does not grant tax sparing credits to developing countries, possibly making U.S. multinationals face a much higher effective tax rate in a developing country than firms from other countries with a treaty including tax sparing credits.

3.5 Implications for Financing Policy

In the face of a high cost of capital for foreign investment financed through equity transfers by the parent, the subsidiary may seek alternative sources of funds. First, parent transfers can be made in debt instead of equity. Since interest payments face lower withholding taxes than dividends in many cases, debt transfer is often a cheaper way of financing the subsidiary.

A more important source of debt financing lies in host countries. Local borrowing, which is ignored by most previous studies on foreign investment, has been an important source of funds for foreign investment. At the end of 1989, the share of local and other foreign borrowing in total external finance for U.S. firms operating abroad was 60.3 percent. The corresponding figure for foreign firms operating in the United States was 71.2 percent.

Column 3 of table 3.3 shows that the cost of capital for foreign investment financed by local borrowing is much lower than that for equity financing regimes. The deduction benefits are proportional to the marginal corporate tax

Table 3.3　　　　**Advantage of Local Financing for U.S. Multinationals**

Host Country	Transfer of Parent Equity (1)	Subsidiary Retained Earnings with Tax Deferral (2)	Local Debt Financing (3)	Tax Cost of Not Using Subsidiary Retained Earnings (1 − 2) (4)	Tax Cost of Not Using Local Debt (1 − 3) (5)
U.S. domestic	7.6	7.6	2.6	0.0	5.0
Japan	10.6	9.0	1.6	1.6	9.0
Canada	9.5	8.1	3.5	1.4	6.0
France	9.7	7.3	3.2	2.4	6.5
Germany	8.3	9.5	0.6	−1.2	7.7
Netherlands	7.8	7.1	2.8	0.7	5.0
United Kingdom	8.6	7.7	3.5	0.9	5.1
Italy	9.9	9.1	1.9	0.8	8.0
Sweden	8.8	7.2	3.6	1.6	5.2
Switzerland	8.2	6.6	3.1	1.6	5.1
Australia	11.5	9.0	3.6	2.5	7.9
Average (foreign investment)	9.3	8.1	2.7	1.2	6.6

rate in a country, and debt financing is particularly attractive in Japan and Germany because of their relatively high corporate tax rates.

Column 5 indicates that the tax cost of not using debt is much higher for foreign investment than for domestic investment. For domestic investment in the United States, the tax cost of using equity financing is 5.0 percent. For U.S. firms operating in Japan, the cost can be as high as 9.0 percent.

In addition, the nontax cost of using debt may be lower for foreign investment than for domestic investment. A multinational may face less risk of default since it can possibly pool relatively independent risks from its worldwide operations and use its combined assets as collateral for loans. Further, foreign borrowing is an important means to hedge against exchange risks associated with foreign-source income.

When borrowing abroad, a U.S. multinational may have an incentive to concentrate its borrowing where tax benefits are large. Japan, Germany, Italy, and Australia are more attractive places for foreign borrowing for U.S. firms than Canada, France, the Netherlands, the United Kingdom, Sweden, and Switzerland as far as taxes are concerned. This observation has become more relevant as integrated world capital markets have narrowed differences in borrowing costs between countries.

If, for some nontax reasons, a U.S. firm has to finance foreign investment using an equity source, subsidiary retained earnings are typically cheaper than parent equity transfers, except in Germany, where split corporate tax rates discriminate against retained earnings (column 4). Note, however, that the cost of capital for investment financed through subsidiary retained earnings reported in this study implicitly assumes that home-country taxes on unrepatriated earnings can be deferred. As mentioned earlier, U.S. firms have limited abilities to defer some of their home-country tax liabilities.

References

Jun, Joosung. 1995. The Impact of International Tax Rules on the Cost of Capital. In *The Effects of Taxation on Multinational Corporations,* ed. Martin Feldstein, James R. Hines, Jr., and R. Glenn Hubbard. Chicago: University of Chicago Press.

Organization for Economic Cooperation and Development. 1991. *Taxing Profits in a Global Economy: Domestic and International Issues.* Paris: Organization for Economic Cooperation and Development.

4 The Importance of Income Shifting to the Design and Analysis of Tax Policy

Roger H. Gordon and Jeffrey K. MacKie-Mason

4.1 Introduction

The academic public finance literature—and the advice academics offer to policymakers—has been dominated by a particular approach to tax analysis. A well-defined tax base is taken as given, and then the scholar studies the effect that taxation of that base has on taxpayer behavior and the distribution of income. For example, if we impose a tax on labor income, by how much are individuals likely to change hours worked? Changes in hours worked in response to tax distortions generate an efficiency loss that must be traded off against any distributional gains from the tax. In order to measure the size of the efficiency loss from labor income taxes, past research has focused on measuring labor supply elasticities.

There is another type of response, however, that is rarely considered. Rather than change work hours in response to taxes, individuals can simply change the way in which their pay is reported for tax purposes in order to reduce tax liabilities. For example, if the corporate tax rate is lower than the individual's personal tax rate, then a self-employed individual can save on taxes by incorporating, retaining his earnings within the corporation where they are taxed at the lower corporate rate, and then bequeathing ownership of the corporation to his heirs so that his earnings entirely escape personal taxes. During his lifetime, his consumption needs can be financed by loans from the corporation, which

Roger H. Gordon is professor of economics at the University of Michigan and a research associate of the National Bureau of Economic Research. Jeffrey K. MacKie-Mason is associate professor of economics and public policy at the University of Michigan and a research associate of the National Bureau of Economic Research.

The authors thank Scott Newlon for comments on a related paper. MacKie-Mason was a visitor at the University of California (Berkeley) Energy Institute while this paper was being written. Financial support for the research reported here was provided in part through National Science Foundation grant SES-9122240.

results in a further reduction in tax liabilities since certain types of interest deductions under the personal tax save more in taxes than are due in corporate taxes on this interest income. Similarly, an employee in a firm can be paid through qualified stock options rather than through wage payments. Under existing tax law, the firm receives no corporate tax deductions in this case, so that the earnings are implicitly taxed at the corporate rate. Personal taxes are due only when the shares are ultimately sold, at capital gains rates, and again these taxes can be avoided entirely if the shares are bequeathed to one's heirs.

This income-shifting response to tax policy has been widely ignored in the past literature, yet this response may be at least as important as changes in real behavior such as hours worked. In a recent paper (Gordon and MacKie-Mason 1995), we incorporated income shifting into a model of labor income taxes, to see its implications for the design of tax policy. We allowed not only for shifting of income between the corporate and the personal tax bases, but also for income shifting between domestic firms and foreign subsidiaries. The results were quite striking. Prior theories of optimal tax design make strong predictions that are inconsistent with most observed tax systems. When we take income shifting explicitly into account, many features of existing tax systems start to make sense. Our success in rationalizing major puzzles regarding current tax policy suggests that income shifting has had an important influence on existing tax policy even if it has been ignored in the academic discussions.

In this paper, we describe our study of the implications of income shifting for tax policy. We summarize the results of the prior literature and describe how they conflict with actual tax policies. We then discuss the pressures placed on a tax system by income shifting between the corporate and the personal tax bases. In contrast to existing theories that predict a zero corporate tax rate, we find an important role for a cash-flow corporate tax at the same rate as the labor tax. Next we discuss the additional pressures that cross-border income shifting between a parent firm and a foreign subsidiary (through transfer pricing and other mechanisms) imposes on tax systems. With the combined effects of domestic and cross-border shifting, we find that we can explain a number of otherwise puzzling features of existing tax codes, including most importantly the very existence of corporate taxes.

4.2   The Role of the Corporate Tax in an Open Economy

A corporate income tax is usually viewed as a supplement to personal taxes on capital income. Existing tax systems attempt to tax the return to savings on equity grounds. But for a variety of reasons, effective tax rates on capital gains are much lower than those on other forms of income from capital. Since much of the income from corporate capital takes the form of capital gains, corporate capital would be tax favored unless the tax system compensates by imposing a separate layer of tax on corporate income.

A number of complications arise in an open economy, however. To begin with, how should the tax system treat income earned by foreigners on capital invested in the country? One clear finding from the theoretical literature (e.g., Gordon 1986; Razin and Sadka 1991) is that a capital income tax should exempt foreign owners if the country is small enough to be a price taker in world capital markets. If the country is a price taker, then any tax on income earned by foreign-owned capital in the country will not be borne by foreigners—foreigners will invest in the country only if the net-of-tax return they earn there is at least as high as what they can get elsewhere. They would continue to invest there in spite of the tax only if the pretax return rises by enough to compensate, which requires that other corporate deductions (primarily wage and rental payments) fall by enough to offset the effects of the tax. This implies that the corporate tax is ultimately borne by domestic workers and landowners. If so, even these groups would be better off if the corporate tax were replaced by direct taxes on wage and rental income. With direct taxes on wage and rental income, capital investment in the country is no longer discouraged, making the country more competitive in world markets.

Another clear prediction from the prior literature is that, if a country's residents are taxed on their capital income, capital income earned at home and abroad should be taxed at the same rate (Razin and Sadka 1991). This generally means that foreign-source income should be taxed when it is earned, rather than when it is repatriated; deferral until repatriation lowers the effective tax rate relative to that on domestic-source income. Further, in order to equate the pre-domestic-tax rates of return from investing at home or abroad, foreign taxes paid should be deductible from foreign-source income (Hamada 1966).

If income from foreign subsidiaries is effectively exempt from domestic taxes, however, as suggested by the evidence in Hines and Hubbard 1990, then the theory concludes that domestic corporate profits should not be taxed—doing so simply drives capital abroad with no compensating benefit. Even if income from foreign subsidiaries is in fact taxed at rates comparable to those on domestic corporate income, if individual investors can effectively escape domestic taxes when they buy financial securities abroad (since the government cannot independently monitor an individual's foreign-source income), then again the theory argues that domestic profits should not be taxed—such taxes simply reduce investment by domestic residents in domestic firms, with no compensating benefits.

These predictions regarding optimal tax policy in an open economy are diametrically opposed to the actual tax laws we observe in most developed countries. Contrary to the theory, most countries have a positive corporate tax rate; they tax foreign-owned corporations; they allow their citizens to defer taxation of foreign-source income until repatriation; and they allow a credit rather than a deduction for foreign taxes paid. Should we conclude that nearly all governments have implemented the wrong policies, and consistently maintained those wrong policies for many years? Or is the theory missing something important?

Not only do the existing theories conflict with actual government behavior, but they also predict that firms should behave differently than they do. For example, multinationals from high-tax countries face a competitive disadvantage in low-tax countries: they pay the same low local taxes as do all firms, but they also pay a high surtax to their home government when they repatriate profits. Yet Hines and Rice (1994) show that U.S. multinationals invest heavily in countries with the lowest tax rates.

Given that multinationals do put subsidiaries in low-tax countries, the standard theories have a clear prediction about the pattern of pretax profit rates on investments in low-tax and high-tax countries. The domestic tax on foreign earnings is postponed until repatriation, so multinationals face lower effective tax rates in countries with lower statutory rates. This implies that the pretax competitive rate of return should be lower in low-tax countries. But Hines and Hubbard (1990) and Grubert and Mutti (1987) find that pretax profit rates of U.S. subsidiaries are *higher* in low-tax countries.

The clear explanation for the above observations is that multinationals are able to shift their accounting profits from high-tax to low-tax countries through transfer pricing, loans between parent and subsidiary, and other devices, thereby reducing their global tax liabilities. The shifted income explains the higher *reported* profit rate in the low-tax countries. The U.S. government's repeated efforts to tighten transfer pricing rules and enforcement, in part through provisions in the 1986 Tax Reform Act that limit income shifting (particularly through interest and R&D allocations), indicate that tax authorities believe cross-border income shifting is an important activity.

Unfortunately, cross-border income shifting alone does not help explain why corporate taxes exist. According to the theory, the mobility of physical capital alone, along with the difficulties in taxing foreign-source income, should be enough to force governments to eliminate taxes on corporate profits. Once we recognize that *accounting* income is also mobile, the tax policies we observe make even less sense. Apparently we need to look yet more closely at what taxpayers are doing.

Our hypothesis is that individuals can easily shift their form of pay so that it is taxed as corporate rather than personal income, just as multinationals can easily shift their internal transactions so that income is taxed abroad rather than at home. As a result of these income-shifting opportunities, we argue below, a corporate tax serves as a backstop to taxes on labor income, thereby enhancing the efficiency of the tax system as a whole. Musgrave (1959) proposed this justification for the existence of a corporate tax, but the idea has been largely ignored since; as a consequence, a number of recent papers argue that corporate taxation should be altogether eliminated.

4.3   Pressures Created by Domestic Income Shifting

If domestic individuals can shift income between the corporate and the personal tax bases, what can we say about the appropriate use of a corporate tax?

Suppose that the prior theories are accepted, so that there are no taxes on corporate income because capital is mobile. Then individuals will have a strong incentive to find ways to report their earnings as corporate income. For example, rather than working as an employee earning taxable wages, an individual could instead become self-employed, incorporate, and accrue income within the corporation free of tax. Alternatively, an employee without entrepreneurial acumen might ask his or her employer for pay in stock options rather than wages, leading under existing tax law to an increase in corporate and a decrease in personal taxable income.

These forms of income shifting lower tax payments, but at a cost. Changing careers from being an employee to being an entrepreneur involves many nontax considerations, while receiving pay through stock options has risk and liquidity implications. As a result, any differences between corporate and personal tax rates not only lead to a loss in tax revenue but also generate efficiency losses.

In a simple model, we have shown the optimal policy response: a cash-flow tax on corporate income at a rate equal to the labor income tax rate.[1] Under such a tax system, individuals can no longer reduce their tax liabilities by changing their form of pay, so would have no tax incentive to pursue costly income-shifting strategies. Such a cash-flow tax would also leave investment decisions undistorted.

As forecast, the corporate tax rate in most countries is very similar to the top personal tax rate, largely eliminating the gain from shifting income from the personal to the corporate tax base. The role of the corporate tax as a backstop for the labor income tax also explains why foreign-owned firms in a country should be subject to the same tax rate as domestic-owned firms, contrary to prior theories. If foreign-owned firms faced a lower rate, then domestic entrepreneurs could easily shelter their earnings by finding a foreign investor to act as a nominal owner of the firm they set up.

A similar argument clarifies another puzzling feature of most international tax systems: why give a credit for foreign taxes paid on foreign-source income, rather than a deduction? First, if foreign-source income were taxed at a lower rate than domestic labor income, then domestic entrepreneurs could reduce their taxes by using their ideas to open subsidiaries abroad rather than at home. By combining this possibility with the previous example in which foreign owners might acquire domestic firms to shift income out of the domestic labor tax base, we can see that subsidiaries would need to be taxed at the maximum of the corporate tax rates prevailing in the host and home countries in order to prevent either form of income shifting. This is precisely what happens under existing crediting schemes.

A number of complications would modify the conclusion that governments

---

1. More specifically, the corporate tax should be coordinated with any personal taxes on corporate income so that the net tax rate on corporate cash flow equals the personal labor income tax rate.

should tax corporate cash flow at the labor tax rate in order to avoid wasteful income shifting. For example, a major activity of entrepreneurs is to develop new ideas. The entrepreneur's private return can differ substantially from the social return, if, for example, others can learn from observing the entrepreneur and use his ideas to compete with him. Thus, inducing the socially optimal level of entrepreneurial activity might require different tax rates on employees and entrepreneurs.

4.4 Pressures Created by Cross-Border Income Shifting

As we mentioned above, there is clear evidence that firms use transfer pricing in order to shift income from high-tax to low-tax locations. What does such cross-border shifting imply for the design of a corporate income tax? We assume that domestic income shifting is also possible, and thus start with a corporate cash-flow tax rate equal to the labor tax rate. Now consider the case of a high-tax home country, with multinationals that own subsidiaries in low-tax host locations. In our model, we assumed that transfer prices were used on inputs purchased by the domestic parent firm from the foreign subsidiary, so ignored transfer pricing of output sold abroad by the domestic parent. In this case, the firm will use too large an accounting price for these inputs, in order to shift taxable income from the high-tax to the low-tax location. The resulting income shifting both lowers domestic tax revenues and creates inefficiencies, because the firm uses too much of the overpriced input in order to reduce tax liabilities and because the effective tax rate on entrepreneurs is now below that on employees.

The home country's efficient policy response is to lower the tax rate at which inputs are deductible, to reduce the incentive to use transfer pricing. We see such a policy response in the income tax rules in the United States, which restrict the amount of deductions a parent firm can take for interest, R&D, and overhead expenses against the U.S.-source income. Another implication of our model is that the corporate tax rate should be somewhat below the labor income tax rate, since use of the corporate tax now introduces additional distortions to those considered previously. In fact, the corporate tax rate in most countries is somewhat lower than the top personal tax rate.

Another policy response to cross-border income shifting is to increase the effective corporate tax rate on foreign-source income, lessening the gain to firms of shifting income abroad. By making the tax rate on foreign-source income equal to that on domestic-source income, the home country could eliminate entirely the incentive to use transfer pricing. Under U.S. tax law, the main difference between the tax treatment of domestic and foreign-source income is that domestic income is taxed year by year, whereas foreign-source income is taxed only at repatriation. One policy response is therefore to tax foreign-source income at accrual, rather than at repatriation.

Much of the gains from this policy change could be achieved by implementing it selectively for income earned in jurisdictions deemed to be tax havens. While some opportunities for transfer pricing would still exist, the main pressures would be eliminated. We see just such a policy in the U.S. subpart F rules that tax passive foreign-source income when it is earned rather than repatriated. A further gain from this policy change is that it reduces countries' gain from being tax havens. Even in tax havens, maintaining low corporate tax rates undermines their domestic taxes on labor income, and would be attractive only if there were enough of a compensating gain through attracting investments by foreign multinationals.

Another policy response to transfer pricing would be to continue to tax foreign-source earnings at repatriation but to lessen the gains from deferral of tax liabilities on foreign-source income. Deferral of taxes on foreign-source earnings is valuable only to the extent that the net-of-local-tax rate of return earned on funds kept abroad is higher than the net-of-tax return available on funds invested at home. If the two rates of return were the same, then there would be no advantage to deferral. If there were no domestic taxes on the return to savings at home, then capital mobility would imply that the net-of-tax rate of return abroad could be no higher in equilibrium than that available at home, eliminating any gain from deferral. Past theoretical work already suggests that capital income taxes should not exist in a small open economy; that capital income taxes increase incentives for transfer pricing only strengthens this conclusion.

4.5   Closing Remarks

Capital mobility between open economies creates strong pressure to eliminate *capital* income taxes. However, this is not the same thing as eliminating *corporate* income taxes. To the extent that individuals can shift their form of pay so that it would be taxed as corporate income rather than as personal wage income, the corporate income tax serves as a backstop to the personal income tax. Incentives to shift income between the corporate and the personal tax bases would be eliminated through use of a corporate cash-flow tax at the same rate as the labor income tax. Cross-border income shifting can be discouraged in a variety of ways, such as modifying the tax treatment of items susceptible to transfer pricing.

We have not attempted in this study to add anything to the discussion concerning whether *capital* income taxes should be used in an open economy. What we do argue is that the primary role of the corporate tax appears to be as a backstop to the personal tax on labor income rather than as a tax on the return to capital invested in the corporate sector. In fact, Gordon and Slemrod (1988) found that U.S. corporate taxable income would increase if we shifted to a cash-flow corporate tax, which in present value exempts capital income, suggesting that the normal return to corporate capital is a minor (in fact negative) component of the existing corporate tax base.[2] Our hypothesis in this paper, consistent with the Gordon and Slemrod evidence, is that reported corporate income is primarily labor income left within the firm to escape personal tax liabilities.

Implicitly supporting the important role of income shifting in the design of tax policy is the fact that many otherwise puzzling aspects of corporate tax systems around the world appear quite sensible once income shifting is taken into account. While it would appear from the nature of government tax policy that income shifting must be important, is there any direct evidence on the importance of income shifting?

While there is a growing body of work documenting the importance of cross-border income shifting within a multinational,[3] there has been relatively little work attempting to measure the extent of income shifting between the corporate and personal tax bases. In related research (MacKie-Mason and Gordon 1993; Gordon and MacKie-Mason 1994), we report evidence that a firm's decision whether to incorporate is significantly affected by tax considerations. This says nothing about the extent of income shifting within an existing corporation, however. Given the systematic downward trend in personal tax rates relative to corporate rates in recent years, if income shifting were important then there should have been a decline in the corporate tax base and an increase in the personal tax base in response to this trend in tax rates. In fact, a number of papers have reported such evidence. For example, Poterba and Auerbach (1987) document a decline in the reported pretax rate of return earned on corporate capital between 1959 to 1985, during which time the difference between the top personal marginal tax rate and the top marginal corporate rate fell from 40 percent to 4 percent. In addition, Feenberg and Poterba (1993) report a sharp jump in the relative income of the richest 0.25 percent of U.S. households in the 1980s, during a period when their personal tax rate fell substantially relative to the corporate tax rate. Our view is that income shifting provides the most plausible explanation for these income trends.

Given that many otherwise puzzling aspects of existing tax policy can be rationalized quite easily if income shifting is important, it would be highly valuable in future research to document the extent and the efficiency costs of income shifting, in order to judge whether the existing policy response to the threat of income shifting is the appropriate one. Since past work has virtually ignored the possibility of income shifting, this would involve a major shift in research effort.

---

2. This study looked at data for only 1983. Subsequent work by Kalambokidis (1992) covering 1975–87 also found that a cash-flow tax base would exceed the existing tax base in all years except 1975.

3. See, for example, Harris et al. 1993.

References

Feenberg, Daniel R., and James M. Poterba. 1993. Income Inequality and the Incomes of Very High-Income Taxpayers: Evidence from Tax Returns. *Tax Policy and the Economy* 7:145–77.

Gordon, Roger H. 1986. Taxation of Investment and Savings in a World Economy. *American Economic Review* 76:1086–1102.

Gordon, Roger H., and Jeffrey K. MacKie-Mason. 1994. Tax Distortions to the Choice of Organizational Form. *Journal of Public Economics* 55:279–306.

———. 1995. Why Is There Corporate Taxation in a Small Open Economy? The Role of Transfer Pricing and Income Shifting. In *The Effects of Taxation on Multinational Corporations,* ed. Martin Feldstein, James R. Hines, Jr., and R. Glenn Hubbard. Chicago: University of Chicago Press.

Gordon, Roger H., and Joel B. Slemrod. 1988. Do We Collect Any Revenue from Taxing Capital Income? *Tax Policy and the Economy* 2:89–130.

Grubert, Harry, and John Mutti. 1987. The Impact of the Tax Reform Act of 1986 on Trade and Capital Flows. In *Compendium of Tax Research 1987.* Washington, DC: U.S. Treasury Department.

Hamada, Koichi. 1966. Strategic Aspects of Taxation on Foreign Investment Income. *Quarterly Journal of Economics* 80:361–75.

Harris, David, Randall Morck, Joel Slemrod, and Bernard Yeung. 1993. Income Shifting in U.S. Multinational Corporations. In *Studies in International Taxation,* ed. Alberto Giovannini, R. Glenn Hubbard, and Joel Slemrod. Chicago: University of Chicago Press.

Hines, James R., Jr., and R. Glenn Hubbard. 1990. Coming Home to America: Dividend Repatriations by U.S. Multinationals. In *Taxation in the Global Economy,* ed. Assaf Razin and Joel Slemrod. Chicago: University of Chicago Press.

Hines, James R., Jr., and Eric M. Rice. 1994. Fiscal Paradise: Foreign Tax Havens and American Business. *Quarterly Journal of Economics* 109:149–82.

Kalambokidis, Laura. 1992. What Is Being Taxed? A Test for the Existence of Excess Profit in the Corporate Income Tax Base. Ph.D. dissertation, University of Michigan.

MacKie-Mason, Jeffrey K., and Roger H. Gordon. 1993. How Much Do Taxes Discourage Incorporation? University of Michigan. Mimeo. Earlier version, NBER Working Paper no. 3781. Cambridge, MA: National Bureau of Economic Research.

Musgrave, Richard. 1959. *The Theory of Public Finance.* New York: McGraw-Hill.

Poterba, James, and Alan Auerbach. 1987. Why Have Corporate Tax Revenues Declined? In *Tax Policy and the Economy,* vol. 1, ed. Lawrence H. Summers. Cambridge: MIT Press.

Razin, Assaf, and Efraim Sadka. 1991. International Tax Competition and Gains from Tax Harmonization. *Economics Letters* 37:69–76.

5   Alternative Minimum Tax Rules and Multinational Corporations

Andrew B. Lyon and Gerald Silverstein

5.1 Introduction

The Tax Reform Act of 1986 established an alternative minimum tax (AMT) for corporations, designed with the intention of preventing corporations from paying low rates of tax on their economic income. Under the rules of the AMT, corporations now calculate their tax payments twice: once using the regular rules of the tax system and a second time using the alternative computation provided under the AMT. Firms pay tax based on the calculation resulting in the greatest liability.

The AMT affects a significant number of firms. In 1990, the corporate AMT accounted for 8.5 percent of corporate tax receipts, or $8.1 billion. Including regular taxes paid by these AMT firms, AMT firms paid 21.4 percent of all corporate income tax. Approximately 25 percent of corporations with assets in excess of $50 million paid AMT. Among the largest firms, those with assets in excess of $500 million, the proportion of firms paying AMT was 30.6 percent.

Among multinational firms, AMT incidence is slightly more prevalent. This is partly due to the correlation between firm size and AMT liability and the fact that the largest firms are also more likely to receive foreign-source income. Among firms in 1990 filing form 1118—the form on which foreign tax credits are calculated—28 percent of those with assets in excess of $50 million paid AMT. Among these multinationals with assets in excess of $500 million, 33.3 percent paid AMT. Of all form 1118 filers, 53 percent of all assets and 56

Andrew B. Lyon is associate professor of economics at the University of Maryland and a faculty research fellow of the National Bureau of Economic Research. Gerald Silverstein is an economist in the Office of Tax Analysis of the U.S. Department of the Treasury.

The authors are grateful to Alan Auerbach, Jim Hines, Glenn Hubbard, and seminar participants at NBER and the Office of Tax Analysis for helpful discussions and comments.

percent of all foreign-source income were accounted for by corporations paying AMT.

Not much is known about how firms are affected by the AMT. Limited past analyses have focused primarily on the incentives *domestic* firms face for undertaking new investment.[1] But the effects of the AMT rules on multinationals are potentially quite different. Multinationals may be affected in a number of different ways, from the design of dividend repatriation strategies to the locational choice for real investment. This paper outlines how multinational corporations' incentives can be affected by the AMT and presents data suggestive of how important these effects may be.

5.2   AMT Provisions Affecting Multinationals

The AMT rules potentially affect multinational corporations (MNCs) in a manner quite different from their effect on domestic corporations. First, the taxable income of domestic corporations (and that of the domestic operations of MNCs) is generally increased due to restrictions on deductions under the AMT and the inclusion of certain income that would be excluded from taxation under the regular tax. For foreign operations, however, deductions are quite similar for AMT and regular tax purposes.

Second, although the domestic tax base is generally larger under the AMT than under the regular tax, the tax rate on all AMT income is 20 percent rather than the 35 percent rate that generally applies to corporations under the regular tax system. As a result, whether a firm pays tax under the AMT depends on the particular sources of income and types of deductions received by the firm. For U.S.-based MNCs, the lower marginal rate of taxation under the AMT may provide the firm a timing opportunity to repatriate income from low-tax foreign countries. Repatriated income is less likely to be subject to U.S. tax, or is subject to a smaller amount of tax, because foreign tax credits can shelter a greater percentage of taxable income.

Third, a separate AMT provision limits the total amount of tax that may be offset through foreign tax credits. For a firm for which this provision is a binding constraint, positive amounts of U.S. tax will be paid on repatriated dividends even if the firm would otherwise have excess foreign tax credits.

The starting point for determining whether a firm owes AMT is the firms' regular taxable income before any deduction for net operating losses. To this amount, the firm adds back a number of deductions that are restricted under the AMT and certain sources of income not taxable under the regular tax rules (adjustments and preferences). Adjustments include a cutback on depreciation allowances allowed for domestic property and a reduction in the preferential treatment of certain assets (such as pollution-control facilities) or benefits for certain industries (such as oil and gas production).

1. See, for example, Lyon 1990, 1991 and references cited therein.

If the firm has deductions for net operating losses, these may offset no more than 90 percent of this computed income (whereas these losses may offset 100 percent of regular income). The resulting income measure is defined as alternative minimum taxable income, which may be reduced by a limited exemption amount.

Tax is calculated by multiplying this net amount by the 20 percent AMT tax rate. Business credits, such as the R&D tax credit, may not be used against the AMT. Tax may be reduced, however, by a limited amount of AMT foreign tax credits, as described in more detail below. This yields the firm's tentative minimum tax. Tentative minimum tax is compared to regular income tax before all credits except the foreign tax credit and the possessions tax credit. If tentative minimum tax exceeds this amount of regular tax liability, the excess is payable as AMT, in addition to the firm's payment of its regular tax liability. Each dollar of AMT payments creates a dollar of AMT credits that may be used in future years only against regular income tax liability. AMT credits may not be used to reduce regular tax liability below tentative minimum tax.

5.3   Investment Incentives of Multinational Corporations

For domestic property, the AMT generally creates a tax penalty for new investment undertaken by an AMT firm, relative to the incentives faced by a regular-tax firm.[2] While income earned under the AMT is taxed at 20 percent, compared to the 35 percent rate of the regular tax system, a firm claims less accelerated depreciation allowances on its domestic investment than for regular tax purposes. In practice, the slower stream of depreciation allowances reduces investment incentives by more than the lower tax rate increases them. For foreign-use property, however, a firm claims the same depreciation deductions on the AMT as it would for regular tax purposes. If the income generated by the foreign investment is taxed currently by the United States, it will be taxed at a maximum rate of 20 percent under the AMT rather than the 35 percent tax rate applying under the regular tax system. As a result, foreign investment incentives appear to be no worse off under the AMT than under the regular tax rules and may, in fact, be improved when the income is currently taxed in the United States.

Calculations for representative categories of equipment confirm this result. For example, for equity-financed investment in equipment located in the

---

2. While firms currently on the AMT are likely to have reduced incentives for domestic investment, the overall effect of the AMT on domestic investment is more difficult to ascertain. This is because the AMT also has an effect on firms that are currently paying regular tax but that anticipate a future period of AMT liability. These firms may have greater investment incentives currently than if they were to remain permanently on the regular tax. See Lyon (1990) for a discussion. The example discussed in the text considers incentives of firms currently subject to the AMT.

United States, the marginal effective corporate tax rate under the regular tax is 26.8 percent.[3] If the firm is on the AMT for five years, the effective tax rate increases to 32.5 percent. For the same firm, if the investment were located abroad and the income generated by the investment were subject to current U.S. taxation, the effective tax rate would decline from 38.3 percent under the regular tax to 36.8 percent under the AMT. This analysis suggests that the AMT creates a *relative* incentive to locate investment abroad rather than in the United States.[4] Domestic investment incentives on the AMT are reduced, while foreign investment incentives are unchanged or improved under the AMT.[5]

5.4   Income Repatriation Incentives

The differences in statutory rates and foreign tax credit calculations create the potential for AMT firms to face different incentives for the receipt of foreign-source income than if they were subject to only the regular tax. Hines and Hubbard (1990), Altshuler and Newlon (1993), and Altshuler, Newlon, and Randolph (chapter 7 in this volume) have shown in other contexts that firms take advantage of deferral and timing opportunities to reduce their global tax liabilities on foreign-source income.

A number of potential tax situations might be considered in evaluating the incentive for dividend repatriation and deferral. The variety of tax situations is somewhat larger under the AMT than for regular tax purposes, because the firm's foreign tax credit position for regular tax purposes—that is, whether it is in excess credit or excess limit—may not be the same as its position under the AMT. In addition, the firm may be in an excess credit position under the AMT due to either the separate income category limitations or the 90 percent

3. The corporate marginal effective tax rate is calculated as $(\rho - s)/\rho$, where ρ is the cost of capital net of depreciation and s is the after-tax real return. The cost of capital for equipment is based on a capital-stock weighted average of the cost of capital for thirty-one types of equipment. Rates of depreciation are based on estimates by Hulten and Wykoff (1981). Annual inflation is assumed to be 3.8 percent, and the after-tax real rate of return is 5 percent. These and other assumptions follow Lyon 1990.

4. Note that for both the regular tax and the AMT, foreign investment receives slower depreciation allowances than for domestic purposes, and, as a result, the effective tax rate for foreign investment is higher under either tax system than for domestic investment. Thus, it is not the case that the AMT creates an *absolute* incentive to invest abroad rather than domestically. Rather, the AMT creates an incentive *relative* to the regular tax system that favors foreign investment over domestic investment.

5. Both foreign and domestic investment incentives may be reduced on the AMT when debt is used to finance investment. Finance costs are higher because interest payments are deductible at the corporate statutory tax rate (35 percent for a regular tax firm and 20 percent for an AMT firm). The after-tax cost of a dollar of interest payments thus rises from 65 cents to 80 cents on the AMT. (The loss in the value of the interest deductions under the AMT serves to increase the AMT credit a firm may claim in the future.) While the absolute cost of investment is increased on the AMT for debt-financed investment, the relative price of foreign investment to U.S. investment is still lower for the AMT firm.

limitation, discussed below, each of which may result in a different incentive for repatriation.

AMT foreign tax credits differ from the foreign tax credits claimed by the taxpayer against regular income tax, although the process of calculating them is similar. Under both the regular tax and the AMT, the foreign tax credit that may be claimed in a given year is limited to the amount of U.S. tax that would have been paid on the foreign income. This limitation is calculated separately for each income category, or "basket."

The U.S. tax that would have been paid on the foreign income is calculated by multiplying (1) the ratio of *foreign income* to *worldwide income* by (2) the taxpayer's *U.S. tax liability* (before use of foreign tax credits). Under the AMT, *foreign income, worldwide income,* and *U.S. tax liability* used in this calculation are all calculated using the AMT rules. The U.S. component of worldwide income will differ from that used in the regular tax computation, chiefly due to the various adjustments and preferences described above. Foreign income will vary to a lesser extent, because the depreciation deductions taken for foreign-use property under the regular tax rules are the same as under the AMT.

After computing the foreign tax credits for each separate limitation category using AMT rules, a second, overall limitation is applied on the amount of foreign tax credits that may be used against AMT. The combined use of deductions for net operating losses and AMT foreign tax credits may not reduce tentative minimum tax by more than 90 percent. AMT foreign tax credits denied due to the 90 percent limitation are treated like other excess foreign tax credits, and may be carried back two years and carried forward five years to offset tentative minimum tax.

The tax incentives for earnings repatriation are considered below for several foreign tax credit positions.

5.4.1 Excess Limit Positions

Consider a firm that is in an excess limit position for both the regular tax and the AMT. Under the regular tax, an additional dollar of earnings repatriations reduces regular tax liability by $T^* - .35$ (assuming the firm is subject to the 35 percent regular tax rate), where T^* is the foreign tax rate. Earnings repatriated from high-tax countries ($T^* > .35$) thus lower current regular tax liability. For a firm on the AMT, tentative minimum tax is reduced by $T^* - .20$ from the additional earnings.

The incentive for earnings repatriation is greater for a firm on the AMT. The reduction in current tax payments is 15 cents larger for the AMT firm than for a regular tax firm. The additional 15-cent saving today comes at a cost of a 15-cent reduction in the AMT credit that could be claimed at a later date. The longer the delay before a firm would be able to use its AMT credits, the greater is the incentive to repatriate earnings while subject to the AMT.

5.4.2 Excess Credit Positions

Under the regular tax, a firm in an excess credit position pays no additional U.S. tax upon the repatriation of foreign income. The stock of foreign tax credit carryovers is affected by repatriation, increasing by $T^* - .35$, where T^* is the foreign tax rate per dollar of income.

Similarly for AMT purposes, assuming the 90 percent limitation is not binding, the additional dollar of earnings repatriations results in no additional AMT, and the stock of AMT foreign tax credits carried to another year increases by $T^* - .20$. In general, for firms in this position, incentives for repatriation are the same for regular and AMT purposes.

If it is alternatively assumed that the 90 percent limitation on the use of foreign tax credits against tentative minimum tax is binding, the cost of repatriating foreign income while on the AMT is increased. This result can occur when the firm has little domestic taxable income (due either to a small U.S. presence, loss carryforwards, or temporarily low domestic profits) and significant amounts of foreign income located in countries with tax rates above the AMT statutory rate. An additional dollar of repatriated earnings increases AMT before credits by 20 cents. Only an additional 18 cents of AMT foreign tax credits may be used to offset this tax, so tentative minimum tax increases by 2 cents. Because current regular tax liability is unchanged by the receipt of this earnings, AMT increases by 2 cents, and a 2-cent AMT credit is generated. AMT foreign tax credits carried to another year increase by $T^* - .18$.

Relative to the case where the 90 percent limitation is not binding, there is a diminished incentive to repatriate earnings. This is true regardless of whether the marginal dividend is from a high-tax country or a low-tax country.

5.4.3 Summary of Repatriation Incentives

When one considers the possibility that the AMT foreign tax credit position of the firm may differ from the foreign tax credit position for regular tax purposes, six possible combinations of tax prices emerge. An analysis of all possible tax price combinations suggests that, in general, the AMT offers firms the opportunity for low-cost earnings repatriations. In only one of the six cases is the AMT tax price greater than the regular tax price for all possible foreign tax rates. This case is where the firm faces the 90 percent limitation on foreign tax credits under the AMT, but for regular tax purposes is in an excess credit position. Even in this case, the firm faces only a 2-cent tax per dollar of repatriated earnings. In four cases, the AMT tax price is less than the regular tax price for some foreign tax rates. In the remaining case, the tax prices are identical.

The next section presents data from tax returns on the extent of AMT liability among multinationals and seeks to examine whether foreign earnings repatriations are influenced by the AMT.

5.5   Tax Return Data of Multinational Corporations

Using Internal Revenue Service tax return information, it is possible to examine the characteristics of multinational corporations paying AMT. Data on the receipt of foreign-source income by these multinationals are examined to explore the possibility that these firms alter their pattern of income repatriation to take advantage of the timing opportunities made possible by the firms' AMT status.

The data used in this analysis are from the 1990 Internal Revenue Service, Statistics of Income microdata files. These files contain data concerning general characteristics of firms, such as assets and tax liabilities, and data relating to foreign-source income and the credit position of firms with foreign tax credits. The data consist of a stratified sample of the corporate population.[6] All corporations with more than $250 million in assets are included in the sample, while corporations in lower asset categories are sampled at a rate varying from 50 percent to 0.25 percent.

5.5.1   AMT Status of Recipients of Foreign-Source Income

Table 5.1 shows AMT incidence for all corporations and for firms claiming a foreign tax credit in 1990 (termed 1118 filers, because such firms claim their foreign tax credits on form 1118). While only 1 to 2 percent of all corporations incur AMT liability, a significantly higher percentage of larger corporations pay AMT. Of corporations with assets in excess of $50 million, 24.6 percent of corporations paid AMT. Among 1118 filers with assets in excess of $50 million, 28.1 percent paid AMT. AMT incidence is even more prevalent among the largest asset category, those with assets in excess of $500 million. Among all corporations in this largest asset category, 30.6 percent paid AMT. Of 1118 filers in this largest asset category, 33.3 percent paid AMT.[7]

Counts of corporations may understate the overall impact of the AMT on economic activity. Because AMT incidence increases with asset size, a larger fraction of total assets is affected by the AMT than suggested by the number of firms paying AMT. Nearly 40 percent of all assets reported by corporations are owned by firms paying AMT. Among 1118 filers, AMT incidence is significantly greater when weighted by assets. Fifty-three percent of assets owned by 1118 filers are owned by those paying AMT. By coincidence, of all assets held by AMT payers, 53 percent of these assets are also owned by 1118 filers paying AMT.

---

6. Pass-through entities such as S-corporations, regulated investment companies, and real estate investment trusts are excluded from this analysis since they are not subject to the AMT.

7. Note that even corporations paying only regular taxes can face the identical incentives as an AMT payer to the extent that they are prevented from using AMT credits or other business credits to reduce regular tax liability below tentative AMT. It is hoped that these firms can be separately identified in later work.

Table 5.1   Counts of Corporations in 1990 by Size, AMT Status, and 1118 Status (in units)

Asset Size Class (thousands of $)	All Corporations			AMT Payers			AMT Incidence (%)	
	Total	1118 Filers	1118 Filers/ Total (%)	Total	1118 Filers	1118 Filers/ Total (%)	All Corporations: AMT Payers/ Total	1118 Filers: AMT Payers/ Total
0–100	1,039,755	324	0.03	1,109	1	0.00	0.11	0.31
100–250	376,082	233	0.06	1,097	0	0.00	0.29	0.00
250–500	236,695	488	0.21	2,329	91	3.89	0.98	18.55
500–1,000	163,416	495	0.30	4,426	42	0.95	2.71	8.49
1,000–10,000	183,975	1,144	0.62	14,297	131	0.91	7.77	11.42
10,000–50,000	25,055	690	2.75	4,482	153	3.41	17.89	22.13
50,000–100,000	5,958	255	4.27	1,335	58	4.35	22.41	22.81
100,000–250,000	4,687	366	7.82	1,101	88	7.98	23.50	24.00
250,000–500,000	1,805	208	11.52	462	54	11.69	25.60	25.96
500,000	2,682	646	24.09	822	215	26.16	30.65	33.28
Total	2,040,110	4,848	0.24	31,459	832	2.64	1.54	17.16

Source: Internal Revenue Service, corporate tax returns and 1118 file, in *Statistics of Income, 1990.*

Another way of representing the importance of the AMT to multinationals is to examine the amount of foreign-source income received by 1118 filers paying the AMT. In total, 56 percent of all foreign-source income is earned by AMT firms. As a result, incentives for the receipt of the majority of foreign-source income are governed by the rules and tax rates of the AMT rather than the regular tax.

5.5.2 The Foreign Credit Position of AMT Taxpayers

As described in section 5.4, the tax price of foreign-source income for AMT firms and the advantage of dividend repatriation while subject to the AMT relative to the regular tax system depends on the foreign tax credit position both for regular tax purposes and for the AMT. As described earlier, six potential tax price differentials exist for a firm subject to the AMT. In table 5.2, the foreign-source income of each 1118 filer is classified into these six AMT cells (and two regular tax cells for non-AMT taxpayers), based on the foreign tax credit position of the firm. Analysis of these different cells gives some indication of how repatriation incentives under the AMT may be affected relative to the regular tax.

As mentioned above, 56 percent of all foreign-source income accruing to corporations claiming a foreign tax credit accrues to AMT-paying firms. As shown in table 5.2, just under half of this amount (27 percent) is earned by firms that are in an excess credit position under both the regular tax and the AMT. Since these firms face the same tax price for the repatriation of foreign-source income on the AMT as they do on the regular tax, their dividend repatriations should not be directly affected by the AMT.

Table 5.2   **Foreign Tax Credit Position of 1118 Filers in 1990 (foreign-source income in millions of $)**

	Position for Regular Taxes		
	Excess Limit	Excess Credit	Total
No AMT liability	22,995	15,777	38,772
	26.01%	17.85%	
Excess limit	4,225	536	4,761
	4.78%	0.61%	
At 90% limit	2,657	15,355	18,012
	3.01%	17.37%	
Excess credit	2,785	24,073	26,858
	3.15%	27.23%	
Total	32,662	55,740	88,402

Source: Internal Revenue Service, corporate tax returns and 1118 file, in *Statistics of Income, 1990.*

A complicating factor to this conclusion is that, as shown in section 5.3, AMT firms have slightly greater incentives to invest in real capital abroad than domestically, relative to the incentives under the regular tax. This could result in a *reduced* incentive to repatriate foreign-source income if funds are retained in the foreign location for reinvestment. Alternatively, there could be an *increased* incentive (relative to the regular tax) to repatriate funds from one foreign location for use in a different foreign location. In this latter case, while measured repatriations would be increased, net repatriations, defined as repatriations net of new transfers abroad, would be lower under the AMT. In future research, we wish to examine information on the foreign subsidiaries of U.S. parents to explore these latter hypotheses.

The next largest cell for AMT taxpayers consists of firms facing the 90 percent limitation on the use of foreign tax credits for AMT purposes, but in an excess credit position for the regular tax. These firms pay an extra tax of 2 cents at the margin for each additional dollar of foreign-source income repatriated relative to their regular tax liability. Approximately 17 percent of foreign-source income is earned by firms facing this 2 percent marginal tax. While the 2 percent tax applies at the margin, inframarginal amounts of foreign-source income may be fully sheltered by foreign tax credits, so total AMT payments are increased by less than the maximum of $307 million (0.02 times $15.35 billion).

Other cells in table 5.2 generate tax savings from repatriations relative to the tax that would be owed under the regular tax. For firms in excess limit under both the regular tax system and the AMT, each dollar of repatriations is subject to 15 cents less current tax than if the regular tax rules applied (.35 − .20). Firms in this cell save approximately $630 million in current taxes, which reduce the AMT credit claimed at a future date by the same amount. Savings can also occur for AMT firms subject to the 90 percent limitation but in an excess limit position under the regular tax. Current U.S. tax payments are reduced to the extent that the average foreign tax rate is less than 33 percent (.35 − .02). Finally, savings also accrue to firms in an excess credit position under the AMT but in excess limit for regular tax purposes. These firms reduce tax liabilities on their foreign source income under the AMT relative to their regular taxes by an amount proportional to the difference between the 35 percent regular tax rate and their average foreign tax credit rate (a number in excess of 20 percent) on each dollar of foreign-source income received.

In sum, it appears that total payments of tax on foreign-source income are lower for the AMT firms than if they were subject to the regular tax rules. The analysis, however, has been unable to determine whether the increased incentive to receive foreign-source income actually significantly affects repatriation behavior. Future research designed to link the parent firm tax returns to information returns filed by the foreign subsidiaries will allow us to better examine how actual payout ratios are affected by the AMT.

5.6 Conclusions

This paper has shown the dimensions along which incentives of U.S.-based multinational corporations may be affected by the AMT. More than half of all corporate foreign-source income in 1990 was received by corporations subject to the AMT. As a result, the tax prices on foreign-source income created by the AMT may be at least as important as those created by the regular tax. While data shown in Gerardi, Milner, and Silverstein (1994) indicate that AMT incidence for the largest corporations in 1990 was approximately 25 percent greater than in 1989 or 1991, the large stock of unclaimed AMT credits accumulated by corporations suggests that the incentives created by the AMT will continue to be an important factor in the future. As shown in section 5.3, the AMT may create a relative incentive for AMT firms to invest abroad rather than domestically. For firms interested in repatriating income from abroad, the AMT may create a temporary timing opportunity that allows repatriation of this income at a lower cost than if the firms were subject to the rules of the regular tax system. These two different incentives may have an ambiguous overall effect on U.S. domestic investment if repatriated income is retained by the parent in the United States. Alternatively, the two incentives together may suggest that the AMT provides an opportunity for firms to repatriate income from foreign locations with poor reinvestment opportunities and reinvest the funds abroad in different foreign locations with better opportunities to take advantage of the temporary, relatively lower cost of capital.

Future research will examine more closely the differences in repatriation behavior between AMT firms and non-AMT firms to determine whether the pattern of repatriation from these subsidiaries is consistent with predictions based on differences in tax prices faced by these firms.

References

Altshuler, Rosanne, and T. Scott Newlon. 1993. The effects of U.S. tax policy on the income repatriation patterns of U.S. multinational corporations. In *Studies in international taxation*, ed. Alberto Giovannini, R. Glenn Hubbard, and Joel Slemrod, 77–115. Chicago: University of Chicago Press.

Gerardi, Geraldine, Hudson Milner, and Gerald Silverstein. 1994. The effects of the corporate alternative minimum tax: Additional results from panel data for 1987–1991. In *National Tax Association—Tax Institute of America: Proceedings of the eighty-sixth annual conference, 1993*, 40–49. Columbus, OH: National Tax Association.

Hines, James R., Jr., and R. Glenn Hubbard. 1990. Coming home to America: Dividend repatriations by U.S. multinationals. In *Taxation in the global economy*, ed. Assaf Razin and Joel Slemrod, 161–207. Chicago: University of Chicago Press.

Hulten, Charles R., and Frank C. Wykoff. 1981. The measurement of economic depreciation. In *Depreciation, inflation, and the taxation of income from capital,* ed. Charles R. Hulten, 81–125. Washington, DC: Urban Institute Press.

Lyon, Andrew B. 1990. Investment incentives under the alternative minimum tax. *National Tax Journal* 43:451–65.

———. 1991. The alternative minimum tax: Equity, efficiency, and incentive effects. In *Economic effects of the corporate alternative minimum tax,* 51–82. Washington, DC: American Council for Capital Formation.

6   Taxes, Technology Transfer, and R&D by Multinational Firms

James R. Hines, Jr.

6.1   Introduction

The technology-related activities of multinational corporations generate interest among policymakers and many others who are concerned about the performance of national economies. Government opinion may be divided over the tactics to use in attracting new technologies, but there is seldom disagreement over the goals of enhancing national productivity through technological development. The statistical evidence generally supports the conclusion that the economic benefits of R&D activity extend to local firms other than those undertaking the R&D.[1] Since there are reasons to expect that externality-generating R&D activities may be underprovided by markets in which developers of new technologies do not capture all of the economic benefits that the technologies provide, various governments offer R&D-related tax subsidies.[2]

James R. Hines, Jr., is associate professor of public policy at the John F. Kennedy School of Government of Harvard University and a faculty research fellow of the National Bureau of Economic Research.

The author thanks Jeffrey Geppert for outstanding research assistance, and Adam Jaffe and James Poterba for helpful comments on an earlier draft. Financial support from the National Science Foundation (grant SES-9209373) and NBER is gratefully acknowledged.

1. See Griliches 1991 and Nadiri 1993 for surveys of empirical measures of productivity spillovers from R&D activities.

2. In theory, the welfare consequences of subsidizing R&D are ambiguous, because competitive pressures might generate too much R&D in certain industries in the absence of a subsidy, and because foreign competitors may benefit from domestic subsidies (or in other ways influence the domestic market). See Dixit 1988 and Reinganum 1989 for surveys of the theory. The United States introduced the Research and Experimentation Tax Credit, and increased the tax deductibility of the R&D expenses of certain multinational corporations, in the Economic Recovery Tax Act of 1981. This legislation appears to have been motivated by consideration of economic externalities, though the focus of congressional sentiment as described in U.S. Congress, Joint Committee on Taxation 1981 is on comparison of U.S. research intensity with the research intensities of other countries.

Governments that do not offer R&D tax subsidies are often concerned that perhaps they should. There are, however, many open questions about the impact of tax policy on the level of R&D.

Tax systems influence the level and content of R&D activity through a variety of channels. This paper focuses on R&D by multinational firms, and the impact of one particular set of taxes: withholding taxes on cross-border royalty payments. Firms that develop new technologies in their home countries and use the technologies in foreign locations are required to pay royalties from foreign affiliates to domestic parent companies. Governments tax these royalty payments. High tax rates make royalties, and the technology imports that they accompany, more expensive for the foreign affiliates that pay the taxes.

In theory, higher costs of imported technology might encourage or discourage local R&D by affiliates of multinational corporations. The difference turns on the nature of production within multinational firms. One possibility is that firms use local R&D jointly with imported technology to produce goods for sale. As an example, it may often be the case that firms need to complement imported technologies with local research efforts that tailor products and processes to local needs. A second possibility is that firms substitute local R&D for imported technologies, as is the case when a certain amount of technological development can be done either at home or abroad.

If local R&D is complementary to imported technology, then high royalty tax rates should discourage local R&D, while if local R&D is a substitute for imported technology, then high royalty tax rates should encourage local R&D.

There are two objectives of the work presented in this paper. The first is to identify the degree to which R&D activity by multinational firms is sensitive to local tax conditions. The second objective is to determine whether imported technology and local R&D are complements or substitutes.

The results suggest that R&D responds significantly to local tax rates, and that local R&D is a substitute for imported technology. These results appear both in the behavior of American investors in other countries, and in the behavior of foreign investors in the United States. Firms appear to react to high royalty tax rates by paying fewer royalties and performing additional R&D locally. To the extent that royalty payments reflect actual technology transfer (rather than adept accounting practices), the behavior of multinational firms implies that local R&D is a substitute for imported technology.

Section 6.2 briefly describes the tax treatment of multinational firms, paying particular attention to technology-related issues. Section 6.3 analyzes the R&D incentives created by international taxation, and describes the data that serve as the basis of the empirical work. Section 6.4 describes the statistical evidence on the reaction of R&D levels to royalty tax rates. Section 6.5 is the conclusion.

6.2   Multinational Firms, Taxation, and International Technology Transfer

This section examines the role of multinational firms in international technology transfer, and reviews the tax treatment of R&D expenditures and royalty receipts by multinational firms.

6.2.1   International Technology Transfer

There is considerable interest in understanding the role that multinational firms play in transferring technologies across borders. There are two methods by which multinational firms provide new technologies to the countries in which they invest. The first method is to develop new technologies locally, through R&D or other similar type of activity. The second method is to import technologies produced elsewhere.

The foreign affiliates of American firms use both methods to bring technologies to the countries in which they operate, and sufficient information exists to assess quantitatively the relative significance of each method. Direct information on the R&D activities of the foreign affiliates of U.S. firms is reported in surveys conducted by the U.S. Commerce Department. Information on technology imports by these affiliates is considerably sketchier. One can, however, infer the approximate magnitude of technology imports from royalties paid by the affiliates to U.S. parent firms and third parties in other countries, since royalty payments should, in principle, reflect the values of imported technologies.

Table 6.1 reports detailed information about the aggregate technology-

Table 6.1   **R&D and Royalty Activity of Foreign Affiliates of U.S. Multinationals**

	1982 (millions of current $)	1989 (millions of current $)
R&D expenditures, total	3,851	7,922
R&D by affiliate for itself	3,073	6,307
R&D by affiliate for others	778	1,615
Royalty receipts, total	435	1,461
From U.S. parents	36	54
From other foreign affiliates	193	656
From unaffiliated Americans	26	97
From unaffiliated foreigners	180	654
Royalty payments, total	4,308	12,472
To U.S. parents	3,663	9,839
To other foreign affiliates	354	1,488
To unaffiliated Americans	102	660
To unaffiliated foreigners	189	485

Source: U.S. Department of Commerce, Bureau of Economic Analysis 1985, 1992.

Note: Data cover majority-owned foreign affiliates of U.S. multinational firms.

related behavior of the foreign affiliates of U.S. firms in 1982 and 1989. It is noteworthy that these affiliates paid more in royalties to their parent firms ($9.8 billion in 1989) than they spent on R&D ($7.9 billion in 1989), though, as the table indicates, there was extensive use of both methods of technology acquisition. The survey distinguishes two categories of R&D expenditure: R&D by affiliates for themselves, and R&D by affiliates for others (the latter of which is R&D performed on a contract basis). R&D by affiliates for themselves constitutes roughly 80 percent of their total R&D expenditures.

American firms spend a considerable amount of money on R&D performed in foreign countries, but in recent years, foreign-owned firms have spent even more than that on R&D performed in the United States. Figure 6.1 illustrates the R&D expenditure levels of foreign affiliates of U.S. firms and foreign-owned firms in the United States over the 1977–90 period. Due to the R&D intensity of the U.S. economy relative to the rest of the world, and the strength of foreign direct investment into the United States since 1973, foreign firms have spent more on R&D inside the United States than American firms have spent on R&D outside the United States in every year since 1982, and the gap between the two expenditure levels is widening.[3]

There is considerable interest in the role of multinational firms in transferring technology across borders, and the impact that government policy can have on the rate and direction of technology transfer. Though these issues have been extensively studied,[4] one of the open questions is the degree to which imported technology is a substitute or complement for local R&D.

6.2.2   The Tax Treatment of R&D Expenditures and Royalty Receipts

The appendix to this volume describes the general features of the U.S. system of taxing the foreign incomes of American corporations. American multinational firms that perform R&D in the United States intending to use the resulting technology both in the United States and abroad face a particularly complex tax treatment of their transactions. Since passage of the Tax Reform Act of 1986, American multinationals are no longer allowed to deduct 100 percent of their U.S. R&D expenses against their U.S. tax liabilities. Instead, U.S. law requires American firms to allocate R&D expenses between U.S. and

---

3. Exchange rate fluctuations can confound the interpretation of figure 6.1, since changes in the value of the dollar relative to foreign currencies affect the dollar-denominated relative magnitudes of R&D performed in the United States and abroad, even if nominal expenditures are unchanged. This consideration is not significant in this case, however, since a simple adjustment for the changing value of the dollar relative to a trade-weighted average of foreign currencies produces a figure that very closely resembles figure 6.1.

4. See, for example, Teece 1976; Germidis 1977; Mansfield, Teece, and Romeo 1979; Mansfield and Romeo 1980; Davidson and McFetridge 1984; Lipsey, Blomstrom, and Kravis 1990; Zejan 1990; Blomstrom 1991; Ethier and Markusen 1991; Wang and Blomstrom 1992; and Blomstrom and Kokko 1993. These studies together consider the effect of a large number of variables on technology transfer and R&D activity, though they do not consider the effect of royalty tax rates on local R&D intensities.

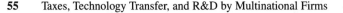

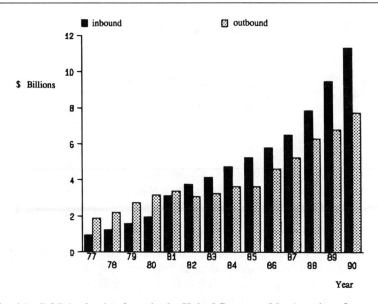

Fig. 6.1   R&D by foreign firms in the United States, and by American firms abroad, 1977–1990

Sources: U.S. Department of Commerce, Bureau of Economic Analysis, various issues; National Science Foundation 1993.

Note: The vertical scale measures billions of current dollars of annual R&D expenditures. Darkly shaded bars represent total R&D expenditures of foreign-owned firms in the United States. Lightly shaded bars represent total R&D expenditures of foreign affiliates of American firms.

foreign sources, based on the fraction of a firm's sales that are foreign.[5] The practical importance of this system is that firms with excess foreign tax credits receive usable tax deductions for only a fraction (equal to the ratio of domestic sales to total worldwide sales) of their U.S. R&D expenses. This system is based on the idea that multinational firms performing R&D in the United States use only a fraction of the output of their R&D activities to enhance their sales in the United States, and consequently, that only a fraction of their R&D costs should be deductible against U.S.-source income.

Royalties received by American parent firms for R&D used abroad represent taxable foreign-source income of the American firms. American firms with deficit foreign tax credits must pay U.S. income tax on these royalty receipts, while firms with excess foreign tax credits can apply the excess credits against U.S. taxes due on the royalties, thereby eliminating the U.S. tax liability created by the royalty receipts.

Most of the world's governments impose withholding taxes on cross-border

5. See Hines 1993, 1994 for descriptions of the precise formulas used and quantitative assessments of their impact on R&D spending levels.

royalty payments from affiliates located within their countries. These royalty tax rates are frequently reduced according to the terms of bilateral tax treaties. For example, the United States imposes a 30 percent tax on royalties paid to foreign corporations, but this tax rate is often reduced, in some cases to zero, when recipients of royalty payments are located in countries with whom the United States has a tax treaty in force.

6.3   Framework and Data

This section analyzes the R&D incentives created by systems of international taxation, and describes the data that serve as the basis of the statistical work.

6.3.1   R&D Incentives

Consider a multinational firm that establishes a foreign affiliate to produce and sell goods in the foreign country in which the affiliate is located.[6] The affiliate generates sales using local inputs of capital, labor, and intermediate products; in addition, the affiliate uses technology from its parent and the technology it generates on its own to produce goods for sale.

American tax law and the tax laws of most other countries require that foreign affiliates pay rents or royalties to their parent firms for the fair market value of technologies transferred from the parent firms to the affiliates.[7] In practice, of course, it is frequently difficult to establish the fair market value of technology transferred from one party to another within a controlled group, since there may exist no market prices for the types of technology in question. In such circumstances, tax-avoiding firms that transfer technology from the parent to its foreign affiliates often have incentives to select royalty payments that transfer taxable income out of high-tax jurisdictions and into low-tax jurisdictions. Governments are aware of this incentive, and try to use their enforcement power to prevent royalties from deviating too greatly from reasonable values.[8]

One way to describe government enforcement efforts is to consider the additional costs that firms bear when royalties deviate from market values. These include costs that firms incur in justifying their royalty declarations to tax authorities. If these adjustment costs rise sufficiently with the deviations of re-

6. This analysis abstracts from the possibility that the activities of foreign affiliates directly enhance the sales of their domestic parent firm. One of the practical difficulties that American firms encounter in such situations is that royalties paid by U.S. parents to their foreign affiliates are severely tax-disadvantaged. See Hines 1994 for a discussion of this issue.

7. Of the twenty-five industrialized countries surveyed by Lawlor (1985), twenty-four apply the arm's-length principle to the taxation of related-party transactions; Hong Kong is the lone exception.

8. For evidence on the overall effectiveness of transfer price enforcement, see Kopits 1976; Grubert and Mutti 1991; Harris et al. 1993; and Hines and Rice 1994.

ported royalties from market values, then they will ultimately limit the degrees to which firms modify royalty payments simply for tax purposes.

Enforcement efforts that require firms to pay royalties equal to market values of technology transfers also mean that taxes on royalty payments should affect the volume of technology transfers. As long as there is a positive relationship between royalty payments and technology transfers, higher royalty taxes raise the cost of transferred technology, and may encourage local firms to undertake their own R&D as a substitute for imported technology.

6.3.2 Data

There are two available sources of detailed information on the R&D activities of multinational firms located in a large number of countries. The first source is the 1989 Benchmark Survey of the Bureau of Economic Analysis (BEA) of the U.S. Department of Commerce. This survey, the results of which are reported in U.S. Department of Commerce 1992, is the most recent comprehensive survey of the activities of the foreign affiliates of American multinational firms. The survey covers activities during 1989. In order to protect the confidentiality of survey respondents, BEA does not divulge the responses of individual firms, and reports country aggregates only for those countries in which there are sufficient numbers of U.S. firms with sizable activities so that aggregate figures do not reveal information about individual firms. Useful R&D and royalty data are available for affiliates in forty-three foreign countries for 1989.

The second source of information is the 1987 survey of foreign direct investment in the United States, reported in U.S. Department of Commerce 1990. This survey describes the activities of foreign-owned firms in the United States during 1987. Due to data suppressions and other limitations, useful data are available on investors from twenty-seven countries during 1987.

The goal of the statistical work is to examine the relationship between royalty tax rates and levels of R&D activity, both for American firms investing in foreign countries and for foreign firms investing in the United States. The difficulty that such a study encounters is that R&D levels differ for reasons that have nothing to do with tax rates. One nontax factor that is clearly associated with R&D spending is the degree of R&D intensity in the countries in which multinational firms have operations. The foreign affiliates of American multinationals located in countries whose economies are R&D-intensive tend to perform more R&D than do affiliates located in other countries. Similarly, foreign-owned affiliates in the United States tend to invest more in R&D if their parent firms are located in technology-intensive countries.

Information is available from the National Science Foundation (1991) on the R&D intensities of a large number of countries. The National Science Foundation constructs indices that reflect national R&D/GNP ratios; due to data limitations, these ratios are not all calculated using data for the same year,

Table 6.2   **R&D Expenditure as a Percentage of GNP, 1961–1989**

	France	West Germany	Japan	United Kingdom	United States
1961	1.4	—	1.4	2.5	2.7
1962	1.5	1.2	1.5	—	2.7
1963	1.6	1.4	1.5	—	2.8
1964	1.8	1.6	1.5	2.3	2.9
1965	2.0	1.7	1.6	—	2.8
1966	2.1	1.8	1.5	2.3	2.8
1967	2.2	2.0	1.6	2.3	2.8
1968	2.1	2.0	1.7	2.2	2.8
1969	2.0	1.8	1.7	2.3	2.7
1970	1.9	2.1	1.9	—	2.6
1971	1.9	2.2	1.9	—	2.4
1972	1.9	2.2	1.9	2.1	2.4
1973	1.8	2.1	2.0	—	2.3
1974	1.8	2.1	2.0	—	2.2
1975	1.8	2.2	2.0	2.1	2.2
1976	1.8	2.1	2.0	—	2.2
1977	1.8	2.1	2.0	—	2.2
1978	1.8	2.2	2.0	2.2	2.1
1979	1.8	2.4	2.1	—	2.2
1980	1.8	2.4	2.2	—	2.3
1981	2.0	2.5	2.3	2.4	2.4
1982	2.1	2.6	2.4	—	2.5
1983	2.1	2.6	2.6	2.2	2.6
1984	2.2	2.6	2.6	—	2.7
1985	2.3	2.8	2.8	2.3	2.8
1986	2.3	2.8	2.8	2.4	2.8
1987	2.3	2.9	2.8	2.3	2.8
1988	2.3	2.9	2.9	2.2	2.7
1989	2.3	2.9	3.0	2.0	2.7

Source: National Science Foundation 1991.

Note: French data are based on gross domestic product (GDP); consequently, percentages may be slightly overstated compared to GNP. Omissions (—) indicate that R&D data are unavailable.

though most observations represent the period 1986–88.[9] In the empirical investigations, the variables that influence R&D demand are interacted with these country-level measures of R&D intensity. This procedure represents a simple, if rather unsubtle, adjustment for differences among countries in the extent to which their firms undertake R&D. Local R&D intensity can have an important impact on the demand for imported technology as well, so the R&D intensity variable appears in the royalty equations.

9. R&D/GNP ratios change little from year to year, as evidenced by the time-series data on France, Germany, Japan, the United Kingdom, and the United States presented in table 6.2 These economies, which are among the most R&D-intensive in the world, exhibit only gradual movements in R&D intensity relative to each other.

Information on tax systems and tax rates is reported by Price Waterhouse (various issues). In the empirical investigations, firms are assumed to face effective tax rates on their technology-related activities equal to statutory corporate tax rates in host countries.

6.4   Responsiveness of R&D Activity to Tax Rates

This section describes the evidence on the responsiveness of R&D activity to royalty tax rates. Two sources of information are considered: information on the behavior of American-owned affiliates in foreign countries, and information on the behavior of foreign-owned affiliates in the United States.

6.4.1   Foreign Affiliates of American Multinational Corporations

Evidence reported in Hines 1995 indicates that American-owned affiliates in foreign countries that tax royalties heavily tend to pay fewer royalties (measured as a fraction of total sales) to their parent firms than do other affiliates. These results control for the technological intensity of host countries in which affiliates are located. The implied elasticity of royalty payments with respect to the royalty tax rate, evaluated at the sample mean, is approximately −0.4. This figure implies that, when royalty tax rates double,[10] royalty payments fall (relative to sales) by 40 percent.

At least part of the responsiveness of royalty payments to local tax rates corresponds to changes in the use of imported technology. The complexity of determining appropriate royalty payments for a variety of intangible property that firms transfer across borders, along with taxpayers' natural incentives to minimize their own tax liabilities, makes reported royalties a somewhat noisy measure of the amount of technology that firms import. Nevertheless, royalty payments should correspond, even if only loosely, to the value of technology imports; the evidence suggests that they respond negatively to higher tax rates.

There are two ways to assess the impact of royalty tax rates on the R&D activities of the foreign affiliates of American multinationals. The first way is to examine the degree to which the ratio of R&D expenses by American-owned affiliates to their labor expenses appears to respond to royalty tax rates.[11] The evidence, reported in Hines 1995, indicates that higher royalty tax

10. The mean royalty tax rate facing the foreign affiliates of American multinationals is 20 percent; hence, doubling the tax rate implies a change from 20 percent to 40 percent.

11. R&D expenditures are scaled by labor compensation in manufacturing. Manufacturing affiliates account for about 90 percent of the foreign R&D activity of multinational firms. Labor compensation is chosen as the denominator because both labor and R&D expenses share the feature of immediate deductibility for tax purposes. Of course, some countries (including the United States) offer tax credits and other inducements to firms that perform R&D (and in some cases to firms that hire labor). A brief survey of country practices indicates, however, that sizable R&D subsidies are rare (for example, see Hall 1993 for an analysis of the magnitude of the marginal subsidy provided R&D in the United States by the Research and Experimentation Tax Credit), and that the primary subsidy comes from the immediate deductibility of R&D expenses that almost all industrialized countries provide.

rates are associated with greater R&D intensities. The estimated elasticity of responsiveness is 0.16, which implies that doubling the royalty tax rate is associated with 16 percent higher R&D expenditures, controlling for other factors (such as the technological intensity of the local economy). Local R&D appears to be a substitute for imported technology.

There is a second way to measure the impact of royalty tax rates on the R&D activities of the foreign affiliates of American multinationals, one that exploits the distinction between total R&D performed by foreign affiliates of U.S. firms and that part of R&D performed by foreign affiliates of U.S. firms for their own use. The latter differs from the former because foreign affiliates of U.S. firms do some R&D on contract for others. Under the assumption that imported technology does not influence R&D performed for other parties, it is possible to compare R&D performed for an affiliate's own use to R&D performed for other parties, in order to infer the impact of royalty tax rates on R&D for own use. The advantage of this technique is that the level of R&D performed for other parties reflects and controls for nontax factors that might otherwise threaten to confound the analysis. The results, reported in Hines 1995, indicate that, once again, local R&D is a substitute for imported technology. The estimated elasticity of responsiveness is now 0.11, which implies that doubling the royalty tax rate is associated with 11 percent higher R&D expenditures, controlling for R&D performed for other parties. This estimated elasticity differs little from the 0.16 elasticity estimated using the first method.

6.4.2   Foreign-Owned Affiliates in the United States

The behavior of foreign-owned affiliates in the United States offers additional evidence on the responsiveness of R&D activity to royalty tax rates. This evidence must, however, be interpreted with caution, owing to heterogeneous circumstances of foreign firms that invest in the United States and the small sample size of twenty-seven foreign countries for which sufficient data are available.

Evidence on the behavior of foreign-owned affiliates in the United States yields conclusions that are very similar to those that emerge from the behavior of the foreign affiliates of American corporations. Foreign investors in the United States pay fewer royalties, and use more R&D-intensive operations, when they face higher tax rates on royalties paid to their home countries. The small number of countries that constitute major foreign investors makes statistical inference difficult, but the estimated coefficients are statistically significant at usual levels of confidence, and in fact, the estimated responsiveness (reported in Hines 1995) is somewhat larger than that for the foreign affiliates of American corporations.

6.5   Conclusion

This paper describes information on the behavior of the foreign affiliates of U.S. firms and foreign-owned affiliates in the United States to estimate the relationship between technology imports and local R&D. The idea is to use the tax treatment of royalty payments to identify the degree of substitutability between these sources of technology. The evidence from the actions of American and foreign firms indicates that R&D responds to local tax rates, and that technology imports and local R&D are substitutes. The substitutability of these technologies carries numerous implications for the design of tax policy toward R&D, particularly when contrasted with the complementarity that is sometimes thought to characterize their relationship.

References

Blomstrom, Magnus. 1991. Host Country Benefits of Foreign Investment. NBER Working Paper no. 3615. Cambridge, MA: National Bureau of Economic Research, February.

Blomstrom, Magnus, and Ari Kokko. 1993. Policies to Encourage Inflows of Technology through Foreign Multinationals. NBER Working Paper no. 4289. Cambridge, MA: National Bureau of Economic Research, March.

Davidson, W. H., and Donald G. McFetridge. 1984. International Technology Transactions and the Theory of the Firm. *Journal of Industrial Economics* 32:253–64.

Dixit, Avinash. 1988. International R&D Competition and Policy. In *International Competitiveness,* ed. A. Michael Spence and Heather A. Hazard, 149–71. Cambridge: Ballinger.

Ethier, Wilfred J., and James R. Markusen. 1991. Multinational Firms, Technology Diffusion, and Trade. NBER Working Paper no. 3825. Cambridge, MA: National Bureau of Economic Research, August.

Germidis, Dimitri, ed. 1977. *Transfer of Technology by Multinational Corporations.* Paris: Organization for Economic Cooperation and Development.

Griliches, Zvi. 1991. The Search for R&D Spillovers. NBER Working Paper no. 3768. Cambridge, MA: National Bureau of Economic Research, July.

Grubert, Harry, and John Mutti. 1991. Taxes, Tariffs, and Transfer Pricing in Multinational Corporate Decisionmaking. *Review of Economics and Statistics* 73:285–93.

Hall, Bronwyn H. 1993. R&D Tax Policy during the 1980s: Success or Failure? In *Tax Policy and the Economy,* vol. 7, ed. James M. Poterba, 1–35. Cambridge: MIT Press.

Harris, David, Randall Morck, Joel Slemrod, and Bernard Yeung. 1993. Income Shifting in U.S. Multinational Corporations. In *Studies in International Taxation,* ed. Alberto Giovannini, R. Glenn Hubbard, and Joel Slemrod, 277–302. Chicago: University of Chicago Press.

Hines, James R., Jr. 1993. On the Sensitivity of R&D to Delicate Tax Changes: The Behavior of U.S. Multinationals in the 1980s. In *Studies in International Taxation,* ed. Alberto Giovannini, R. Glenn Hubbard, and Joel Slemrod, 149–87. Chicago: University of Chicago Press.

———. 1994. No Place Like Home: Tax Incentives and the Location of R&D by American Multinationals. In *Tax Policy and the Economy,* vol. 8, ed. James M. Poterba, 65–104. Cambridge: MIT Press.

———. 1995. Taxes, Technology Transfer, and the R&D Activities of Multinational Firms. In *The Effects of Taxation on Multinational Corporations,* ed. Martin Feldstein, James R. Hines, Jr., and R. Glenn Hubbard. Chicago: University of Chicago Press.

Hines, James R., Jr., and Eric M. Rice. 1994. Fiscal Paradise: Foreign Tax Havens and American Business. *Quarterly Journal of Economics* 109:149–82.

Kopits, George F. 1976. Intra-Firm Royalties Crossing Frontiers and Transfer-Pricing Behaviour. *Economic Journal* 86:791–805.

Lawlor, William R., ed. 1985. *Cross-Border Transactions between Related Companies: A Summary of Tax Rules.* Deventer, The Netherlands: Kluwer.

Lipsey, Robert E., Magnus Blomstrom, and Irving B. Kravis. 1990. R&D by Multinational Firms and Host Country Exports. In *Science and Technology: Lessons for Development Policy,* ed. Robert E. Evenson and Gustav Ranis, 271–300. Boulder, CO: Westview Press.

Mansfield, Edwin, and Anthony Romeo. 1980. Technology Transfer to Overseas Subsidiaries by U.S.-Based Firms. *Quarterly Journal of Economics* 95:737–50.

Mansfield, Edwin, David J. Teece, and Anthony Romeo. 1979. Overseas Research and Development by U.S.-Based Firms. *Economica* 46:187–96.

Nadiri, M. Ishaq. 1993. Innovations and Technological Spillovers. NBER Working Paper no. 4423. Cambridge, MA: National Bureau of Economic Research, August.

National Science Foundation. 1991. *International Science and Technology Data Update: 1991.* NSF 91-309. Washington, DC: National Science Foundation.

———. 1993. *Selected Data on Research and Development in Industry: 1991.* Washington, DC: National Science Foundation.

Price Waterhouse. Various issues. *Corporate Taxes: A Worldwide Summary.* New York: Price Waterhouse.

Reinganum, Jennifer F. 1989. The Timing of Innovation: Research, Development, and Diffusion. In *Handbook of Industrial Organization,* vol. 1, ed. Richard Schmalensee and Robert D. Willig. Amsterdam: North-Holland.

Teece, David J. 1976. *The Multinational Corporation and the Resource Cost of International Technology Transfer.* Cambridge: Ballinger.

U.S. Congress. Joint Committee on Taxation. 1981. *General Explanation of the Economic Recovery Tax Act of 1981.* Washington, DC: Government Printing Office.

U.S. Department of Commerce. Bureau of Economic Analysis. Various issues. *Foreign Direct Investment in the United States.* Washington, DC: Government Printing Office.

———. 1985. *U.S. Direct Investment Abroad: 1982 Benchmark Survey Data.* Washington, DC: Government Printing Office.

———. 1990. *Foreign Direct Investment in the United States: 1987 Benchmark Survey, Final Results.* Washington, DC: Government Printing Office.

———. 1992. *U.S. Direct Investment Abroad: 1989 Benchmark Survey, Final Results.* Washington, DC: Government Printing Office.

Wang, Jian-Ye, and Magnus Blomstrom. 1992. Foreign Investment and Technology Transfer: A Simple Model. *European Economic Review* 36:137–55.

Zejan, Mario C. 1990. R&D Activities in Affiliates of Swedish Multinational Enterprises. *Scandinavian Journal of Economics* 92:487–500.

7   Tax Planning, Timing Effects, and the Impact of Repatriation Taxes on Dividend Remittances

Rosanne Altshuler, T. Scott Newlon,
and William C. Randolph

7.1   Introduction

The U.S. system for taxing the income earned by the foreign subsidiaries of
U.S. corporations defers taxation of foreign income until it is brought back to
the United States and provides a credit for foreign taxes paid.[1] Under this credit
and deferral system, the two main forms of repatriation tax that a firm incurs
on income remitted from a foreign subsidiary are the residual home-country
tax liability (if any) not offset by the foreign tax credit, and any withholding tax imposed by the source country. An open question in the literature on
the taxation of multinational corporations is, do these repatriation taxes influence whether the profits of foreign subsidiaries are repatriated or reinvested
abroad?

Theoretical arguments by Hartman (1985) suggest that, under a credit and
deferral tax system, the repatriation tax on foreign-source income is irrelevant
to the investment and dividend payment decisions of foreign subsidiaries that
are financed through retained earnings ("mature" subsidiaries). Hartman's insight was that, since the repatriation tax is unavoidable, it reduces the opportunity cost of investment and the return to investment by the same amount. As a
result, the tax does not affect a mature subsidiary's choice between reinvesting

Rosanne Altshuler is assistant professor of economics at Rutgers University and a faculty research fellow of the National Bureau of Economic Research. T. Scott Newlon is an economist in
the Office of Tax Analysis of the U.S. Department of the Treasury. William C. Randolph is an
economist in the Congressional Budget Office.

The authors are very grateful to Gordon Wilson for his assistance in using the Treasury tax data.
Any views expressed in this paper are those of the authors and do not necessarily represent those
of the U.S. Treasury Department or the Congressional Budget Office.

1. The subpart F provisions of the tax code provide for accrual-basis taxation on certain foreign income.

its foreign earnings and repatriating funds to its parent.[2] The results of recent empirical work that used cross-sectional data on U.S. multinationals seem to contradict this result.[3] These studies indicate that dividend remittances are sensitive to repatriation taxes. This presents a puzzle.

Hartman's analysis is based on the assumption that taxes on dividends are constant over time. In a recent study (Altshuler, Newlon, and Randolph 1995), we find that the empirical evidence can be reconciled with the theoretical results by recognizing that repatriation taxes on dividends may vary over time. This variability provides firms with an incentive to repatriate relatively more profits from a subsidiary when the tax cost of repatriation is temporarily low relative to the expected future tax cost. Likewise, they would retain more profits when the tax cost of repatriation is higher than the expected future tax cost. Such timing behavior would cause studies that use cross-sectional data to find a relationship between dividend payout levels and the current tax cost of dividend payments. However, the actual relationship would be between dividend payout levels and the current level of the tax cost *relative* to its expected future level.

If timing opportunities are important to dividend payout decisions, then it becomes difficult to interpret the tax effects estimated in previous papers. By using the current tax price of dividend repatriations as an explanatory variable, these estimates will tend to confuse the effects of permanent changes in current and future repatriation taxes, as would occur due to changes in statutory tax rates, with the effects of tax changes due to transitory changes in the situation of the taxpayer. In Altshuler, Newlon, and Randolph 1995, hereafter A-N-R, we use a data set containing U.S. tax return information for a large sample of U.S. corporations and their foreign subsidiaries to estimate separate effects for the permanent and transitory components of the tax price of dividend repatriation. We find that the permanent tax price effect is significantly different from the transitory price effect and is not significantly different from zero, while the transitory tax price effect is negative and significant. Our results imply that the

---

2. Note that this result does not imply that home- and host-country taxes have no effect on the repatriation decision. They do have an impact due to their effect on home- and host-country after-tax rates of return, but not through the tax on repatriation. This analysis is essentially an application of the "new view" or "tax capitalization view" of dividend taxation put forward by King (1977), Auerbach (1979), and Bradford (1981). The "new view" holds that taxes on dividends (if constant over time) have no distortionary effects on the real decisions of domestic corporations. Although Hartman's analysis pertains to the residual U.S. tax on foreign income, it applies equally well to withholding taxes.

3. Mutti (1981) found significant tax effects in estimates of the parameters of a dividend equation using U.S. tax return data from 1972. Hines and Hubbard (1990) used 1984 tax return data of a large sample of U.S. corporations and their foreign subsidiaries and found significant evidence of tax effects on income repatriation. Altshuler and Newlon (1993) used U.S. tax return data from 1986 to investigate tax effects on dividend remittances from foreign subsidiaries to their U.S. parent corporations. This paper improved upon previous work by providing a more accurate specification of the tax incentives facing firms. Results from estimates of dividend equations indicated a somewhat larger and more significant tax effect than had been previously estimated.

previous empirical work has measured the effect of timing behavior and does not, therefore, contradict the prediction of Hartman's model.

This paper summarizes the research methodology and results of A-N-R. Section 7.2 briefly discusses the tax consequences of dividend repatriations and explains how the tax consequences can vary over time. The econometric method used to separate permanent from transitory tax price effects is presented in section 7.3. The data set is briefly described and results are summarized in section 7.4. The policy implications of this work are discussed in the final section of the paper.

7.2   The Tax Price of Dividend Repatriations

We define the tax price of a dividend remittance as the additional global tax liability arising from an incremental dollar's worth of dividend repatriations. To derive the tax price, we must take into account both the incremental U.S. and source-country taxes on a dollar of dividends. The appendix to this volume describes the general features of U.S. taxation of the foreign income of multinational corporations. The foreign tax credit generated by a dividend remittance from a foreign subsidiary is calculated by grossing up the dividend to reflect foreign taxes deemed paid on the income underlying the dividend.[4] Suppose that subsidiary i makes a dividend payment, D_i, to its parent corporation. The grossed-up dividend is

$$(1) \qquad D_i + T_i D_i/(Y_i - T_i),$$

where T_i denotes the total foreign income tax paid by subsidiary i and Y_i denotes the subsidiary's pretax income from the U.S. perspective. Equation (1) can be rewritten as $D_i/(1 - \tau_i)$, where τ_i represents the average subsidiary tax rate, T_i/Y_i, on foreign earnings from the U.S. perspective. The U.S. tax on the dividend before credits is $\tau D_i/(1 - \tau_i)$, where τ denotes the U.S. rate of tax. The foreign taxes creditable against U.S. tax liability are deemed-paid taxes plus withholding taxes, or

$$(2) \qquad \tau_i D_i/(1 - \tau_i) + \omega_i D_i,$$

where ω_i denotes the withholding tax rate in the host country. If the parent has excess credits, any U.S. tax liability on a dollar of dividends is offset by the foreign tax credit. If the parent has excess limitation, the U.S. tax liability equals

$$(3) \qquad (\tau - \tau_i)D_i/(1 - \tau_i) - \omega_i D_i.$$

---

4. For tax years beginning in 1987, the amount of foreign tax credit associated with a dividend payment is based on the accumulated value of earnings and profits. Although this changes the gross-up formula in the text, it is not relevant for our analysis, since our data is taken from years prior to 1987.

To compute the global tax price, we add the source-country effect to the U.S. tax effect. Under a classical corporate income tax system, the only host-country tax consequences of a dividend remittance are the associated withholding taxes.[5] If the parent has excess credits, there is no U.S. tax consequence, and therefore the global tax price is ω_i. Otherwise, the parent is in excess limitation, and the global tax price is $(\tau - \tau_i)/(1 - \tau_i)$.[6] As indicated in the appendix to this volume, the foreign tax credit limitation operates to some extent on an overall basis. This means that excess credits accruing from one source of foreign income can often be used to offset U.S. tax (excess limitation) on foreign income from another source. As a result, the effect of repatriating foreign income from a particular source may be positive, negative, or zero.[7]

There are at least two different ways in which the tax price described above may vary over time. First, it may vary due to differences between the tax-base definitions of the United States and the host country of the foreign subsidiary. As mentioned above, the U.S. foreign tax credit is based on the average foreign tax rate of subsidiary, where the average is calculated with respect to the U.S. definition of the tax base. Differences in tax-base definitions may vary over time, for example, if capital-cost allowances differ, causing the average foreign tax rate as defined by the United States to vary. This variation causes the foreign tax credit allowed for a given dividend payment to vary over time as well. Such variations in the average foreign tax rate may be planned. For example, to the extent that the timing of deductions and credits is discretionary, a foreign subsidiary may shift them from years in which it is remitting income to years in which it is not remitting income, thereby maximizing the foreign tax credit and minimizing the tax price of repatriation.[8]

---

5. For simplicity, we focus our discussion in this section on the derivation of the tax price of a dividend remittance from a foreign subsidiary operating in a country that uses a classical corporate tax system. In our empirical work, we also take details of host-country tax systems into account, since our sample includes subsidiaries that operate in countries with split-rate and imputation systems. The derivations of the tax prices for these types of tax systems are discussed in detail in Altshuler and Newlon 1993.

6. We neglect here the cases in which the parent corporation has tax losses, since, as in earlier papers by Hines and Hubbard (1990) and Altshuler and Newlon (1993), we include in our sample only those U.S. corporations with positive worldwide taxable income. They are excluded here for simplicity's sake, since the carryover rules for tax losses and foreign tax credits can interact in ways that may complicate the incentives for income repatriation of these firms.

7. This is called cross-crediting or averaging of foreign income. Congress has restricted cross-crediting by creating *baskets* of different types of foreign income, to each of which a separate foreign tax credit limitation applies. Before the 1986 Tax Reform Act, the period that our study covers, there were five separate baskets: (1) investment interest income, (2) domestic international sales corporation dividend income, (3) the foreign trade income of a foreign sales corporation, (4) distributions from a foreign sales corporation, and (5) all other foreign-source income, which we will call general limitation income. The act decreased the potential for cross-crediting further by increasing the number of separate limitation baskets to nine.

8. The method was a more useful tax-planning device for U.S. multinationals prior to the Tax Reform Act of 1986, when the foreign tax credit was calculated year by year. The act switched to a system in which the foreign tax credit is calculated based on the pool of previously unremitted

The second cause of variation in the tax price is movement, over time, by the parent company between the two foreign tax credit positions of excess credit and excess limitation. As explained above, the tax price differs between the two situations.[9]

7.3   An Empirical Model of Dividend Repatriations

Previous work has estimated a simple regression model of dividend repatriations.[10] For subsidiaries that pay a dividend, the model takes the following basic form:

$$(4) \qquad d = a_0 + a_1 P + br + XA + \varepsilon,$$

where d is the dividend payout, expressed as the ratio of subsidiary dividends to assets; P is the current tax price of dividend repatriation;[11] r is the after-tax rate of return for the subsidiary; and X represents several variable characteristics of the subsidiaries and parents, the most important of which is the age of the subsidiary.[12]

By using the current tax price, P, the above model may confound the potentially different effects of permanent and transitory components of the tax price and overestimate the effect of the permanent component.[13] Our empirical model generalizes equation (4) to allow for differences in transitory and permanent tax price effects:

$$(5) \qquad d = a_0 + a_1(P - P^*) + a_2 P^* + br + XA + \varepsilon,$$

where P^* is the permanent component of the tax price, and hence $(P - P^*)$ is the transitory component.[14] We estimate the model in a slightly different form:

---

foreign earnings and uncredited taxes, and, therefore, shifting the year in which tax credits and deductions are taken has much less effect on the foreign tax rate for U.S. foreign tax credit purposes.

9. Altshuler and Newlon (1993) found that a significant proportion of U.S. multinationals switched credit positions during the 1980s.

10. See Hines and Hubbard 1990; Altshuler and Newlon 1993.

11. Altshuler and Newlon (1993) also use a measure of the "expected" tax price that attempts to take into account the fact that excess foreign tax credits can be carried back to several prior years or forward to several future years to offset taxes in those years.

12. Some theoretical literature (such as Newlon 1987 and Sinn 1990) suggests that older subsidiaries should have higher dividend payout ratios. This prediction is a direct consequence of the value of deferral when there is a repatriation tax; that is, if there is deferral, then dividend payouts will on average be an increasing function of age, other things constant.

13. In particular, a transitory decrease (increase) in the tax price reduces the current tax price relative to future tax prices, and thus enables the firm to increase the value of its foreign source income by accelerating (delaying) dividend repatriations. But a permanent change in the tax price does not change the relative prices of current and future repatriation. Therefore, one would expect dividend repatriations to be affected more by transitory than by permanent changes in tax prices.

14. In using "permanent" and "transitory," we are adopting a convenient shorthand for talking about the expected future tax price and how it differs from the current tax price. Note that the expected future tax price may change over time, so it is not really permanent. Holding the transi-

(6) $d = a_0 + a_1 P + (a_2 - a_1)P^* + br + XA + \varepsilon.$

One difficulty in estimating equation (6) is that the permanent component of the tax price, P^*, is not observed. To capture the effect of P^*, we use an instrumental variables approach in which we instrument the tax price on a variable, P^i, that we expect to be correlated with the permanent component of the tax price but uncorrelated with its transitory component. This essentially involves replacing P^* in equation (6) with its predicted value,

$$\hat{P}^* = \hat{b}_0 + \hat{b}_1 P^i + \hat{b}_2 r + X\hat{B},$$

where the coefficients are derived from the regression

$$P^* = b_0 + b_1 P^i + b_2 r + XB + \xi.$$

In this paper, we use the country average tax price as an instrument for the permanent component of the tax price.[15] By using this method, we have assumed that variations in country average repatriation tax prices will be correlated with the permanent component of tax price variation, but uncorrelated with transitory variations.[16] In other words, the future tax price of repatriation from a particular subsidiary would be expected to be higher if the average price is higher when measured across all subsidiaries located in the same country. Because the average for each country is always calculated across more than twenty-five subsidiaries, regardless of whether dividends are paid from each subsidiary, the average would not depend on any particular parent's temporary credit position or any particular subsidiary's temporary level of the foreign effective tax rate used for calculation of the foreign tax credit. In A-N-R, we also experiment with using the statutory withholding tax rate as an instrument for the permanent tax price component.

7.4   Results

The data are described in more detail in A-N-R. Briefly, the data are derived from corporate income tax returns (1120 forms), the forms filed in support of foreign tax credit claims (1118 forms), and the information returns filed for each foreign subsidiary controlled by a U.S. corporation (5471 forms). These data allowed us to match subsidiary-specific information on dividend remit-

---

tory component constant, however, the coefficient of P^* allows us to predict the effect of a permanent change in the tax price. This is why it is called the permanent price.

15. Our estimation strategy is similar to that of Burman and Randolph (1994), who used state tax rates as instruments to separate permanent from transitory effects of taxes on capital gains realizations.

16. We demonstrate that there is substantial variation across countries in mean tax prices in table 1 of A-N-R. We argue that the degree of variation we found across countries suggests that the average country tax price is a useful instrument, since the cross-country variation is presumably correlated with variation in the permanent component of the tax price.

tances and other financial variables with parent tax return information.[17] Detailed data from foreign tax credit forms and data from 5471 forms were available only in years 1980, 1982, 1984, and 1986. After applying several screens to the data to eliminate observations for which the data were deemed unreliable, we were left with a sample of 22,906 subsidiary-specific observations.

Table 7.1 presents our main estimation results. We use a Tobit procedure for our estimation to account for the fact that only 28 percent of the subsidiaries pay any dividends. Column 1 presents the results of estimating the simple dividend model presented in equation (4), which incorporates only the current tax price of repatriation. These results are similar to those found in previous work.[18] The coefficient of the current tax price is negative, statistically significant, and of similar magnitude to the estimates in previous papers.[19]

Column 2 presents the results of estimating the model in equation (6), which distinguishes between permanent and transitory tax price effects. To interpret the tax price coefficient estimates, recall that in equation (6) the effect of the transitory component of the tax price is captured by the coefficient of the current tax price, while the coefficient of the permanent tax price equals the difference between the effects of permanent and transitory changes in the tax price. Thus, for column 2, the coefficient estimates in the first row of the table represent transitory tax price effects, the second-row coefficient estimates represent the difference between the permanent and transitory tax price effects, and the coefficient estimates in the third row, which are sums of the coefficients in the first two rows, represent permanent tax price effects.

The estimated effect of the transitory component of the tax price (in the first row) is negative and statistically significant. Furthermore, it is larger in absolute magnitude than the estimated effect from the model excluding the permanent tax price effect.[20] This result implies that transitory variation in the tax price has a large effect on the incentive to repatriate income.

The estimated difference between the permanent and transitory tax price effects presented in the second row of column 2 is positive and statistically significant. This implies that the permanent component of the tax price not only is significantly different from the transitory tax price effect but also, since the coefficient is positive, cannot have as large a negative impact on dividend repatriations. In fact, the estimated permanent tax price effect presented in the

17. These data were supplemented by withholding tax rate information taken from the Price Waterhouse tax guides and tax treaties.

18. See Hines and Hubbard 1990; Altshuler and Newlon 1993.

19. To gauge the economic significance of this coefficient, note that it implies that a reduction in tax price of one standard deviation (0.34) implies an increase in the overall dividend payout ratio (including those that pay dividends and those that do not) of about 0.004, which is equal to about 11 percent of the mean dividend payout ratio of 0.036. Thus, moving the tax price from one standard deviation above the mean to one standard deviation below the mean implies an increase in the dividend payout ratio equal to about 22 percent of the mean dividend payout ratio.

20. A Hausman test shows that this difference is statistically significant.

Table 7.1   Tobit Model Estimation Results (dependent variable: subsidiary dividends over assets)

Right-hand Variables, Estimation Details	Without Permanent Tax Price	With Permanent Tax Price
Current (global) tax price	−0.046	−0.059
	(.0057)	(.0062)
Permanent tax price[a]	—	0.087
		(.016)
Sum of tax price coefficients[b]	—	0.027
		(0.015)
Subsidiary earnings/assets	0.58	0.55
	(.016)	(.016)
Subsidiary age/100	0.37	0.38
	(.017)	(.017)
Intercept (1980)	−0.29	−0.29
	(.0059)	(.0060)
1982 dummy	0.026	0.026
	(.0051)	(.0051)
1984 dummy	−0.029	−0.030
	(.0053)	(.0053)
1986 dummy	−0.012	−0.012
	(.0065)	(.0065)
Observations	22,906	22,906
Paying dividends (%)	28	28

Note: Standard errors in parentheses.

[a]Measures the difference between effects of changes in permant and transitory tax prices (transitory tax price = current tax price − permanent tax price).

[b]Measures the effect of permanent tax price changes, holding the transitory tax price constant.

third row is not significantly different from zero. These results provide support for the hypothesis that the dividend repatriation incentive is affected by transitory but not permanent changes in the tax price of repatriation.

In A-N-R, we also present the results from a series of estimation experiments designed to test the specification and methods underlying the results shown in column 2. One test provides evidence that further supports our claim that the coefficient of the current tax price measures only responses to transitory price changes. For this experiment, we use two-year changes in the tax prices for each subsidiary to construct an instrumental variable for the current tax price. We find that the results are essentially the same as in column 2. In another specification test, we find that our main results are essentially unchanged whether we use country average tax prices, as in column 2, or country withholding tax rates to construct instruments for the permanent component of the tax price. This test provides a stronger test of, but does not reject, the fundamental prediction from Hartman's model, because the withholding tax is purely a repatriation tax, whereas the country average tax prices may also vary as a result of international differences in effective tax rates on corporate income.

7.5   Conclusions and Policy Implications

Our results suggest that the tax price effects on dividend repatriations found in previous studies using the simple model of dividend repatriations apparently measure largely the effect of the timing of dividend repatriations designed to take advantage of intertemporal variation in tax prices. These timing opportunities may arise either endogenously, through tax planning that affects both tax prices and dividend payments, or through exogenously caused variations in tax prices. Therefore, although repatriation taxes seem to affect dividend repatriation behavior, this is apparently only because tax prices vary over time. The observed behavior is thus reconciled with the prediction of Hartman's model.

The results presented here should not be construed to imply that the "permanent" levels of host and home-country income taxation do not affect dividend repatriation by foreign subsidiaries. As predicted by our results, host- and home-country corporate taxation will affect the earnings reinvestment decision, and hence the dividend repatriation decision, through their impacts on host- and home-country after-tax rates of return. The evidence from our study implies that host- and home-country taxation do not have any additional effect on repatriation through the permanent component of the repatriation tax.

These results may have policy implications. The most obvious implications relate to policies on dividend withholding tax rates. For example, many capital-importing countries have considered lowering withholding taxes, either unilaterally or in the context of bilateral tax treaty negotiations, to try to attract new equity investment. But some countries may have been inhibited by the fear that such a measure would lead to increased flight of the accumulated multinational equity "trapped" by existing high withholding taxes. According to our results, such fears are unfounded as long as the reduction in the withholding tax rate is viewed as permanent. Permanent changes in dividend withholding tax rates appear more likely to affect decisions about new equity investment, and do not appear to affect repatriation of equity accumulated from past earnings.[21]

To the extent that our results are consistent with the Hartman model, they have implications regarding the incentive effects of the credit and deferral system that the United States uses to tax most foreign income of U.S. multinationals. In particular, if the repatriation tax does not affect the decision to repatriate dividends, then, at least as with regard to retained earnings, the incentives for

---

21. If a reduction in withholding tax rates is perceived by multinational investors as a signal of more favorable and stable policies toward multinational investment, it may in fact increase reinvestment of earnings.

forcign investment out of foreign retained earnings are the same as they would be under a system that exempts foreign income from taxation.

References

Altshuler, Rosanne, and T. Scott Newlon. 1993. The Effects of U.S. Tax Policy on the Income Repatriation Patterns of U.S. Multinational Corporations. In *Studies in International Taxation,* ed. Alberto Giovannini, R. Glenn Hubbard, and Joel Slemrod, 77–115. Chicago: University of Chicago Press.

Altshuler, Rosanne, T. Scott Newlon, and William C. Randolph. 1995. Do Repatriation Taxes Matter? Evidence from the Tax Returns of U.S. Multinationals. In *The Effects of Taxation on Multinational Corporations,* ed. Martin Feldstein, James R. Hines, Jr., and R. Glenn Hubbard. Chicago: University of Chicago Press.

Auerbach, Alan J. 1979. Wealth Maximization and the Cost of Capital. *Quarterly Journal of Economics* 93:433–46.

Bradford, David. 1981. The Incidence and Allocation Effects of a Tax on Corporate Distributions. *Journal of Public Economics* 15:1–22.

Burman, Leonard, and William C. Randolph. 1994. Distinguishing Permanent from Transitory Effects of Capital Gains Tax Changes: New Evidence from Micro Data. *American Economic Review* 84(4):794–809.

Hartman, David. 1985. Tax Policy and Foreign Direct Investment, *Journal of Public Economics* 26:107–21.

Hines, James R., Jr., and R. Glenn Hubbard. 1990. Coming Home to America: Dividend Repatriations by U.S. Multinationals. In *Taxation in the Global Economy,* ed. Assaf Razin and Joel Slemrod, 161–200. Chicago: University of Chicago Press.

King, Mervyn. 1977. *Public Policy and the Corporation.* London: Chapman and Hall.

Mutti, John. 1981. Tax Incentives and Repatriation Decisions of U.S. Multinational Corporations. *National Tax Journal* 34:241–48.

Newlon, T. Scott. 1987. Tax Policy and the Multinational Firm's Financial Policy and Investment Decisions. Ph.D. dissertation, Princeton University.

Price Waterhouse. 1980, 1982, 1984, 1986. *Corporate Taxes: A Worldwide Summary.* New York: Price Waterhouse.

Sinn, Hans Werner. 1990. Taxation and the Birth of Foreign Subsidiaries. NBER Working Paper no. 3519. Cambridge, MA: National Bureau of Economic Research, November.

8 Is Foreign Direct Investment Sensitive to Taxes?

Jason G. Cummins and R. Glenn Hubbard

8.1 Introduction

Understanding the determinants of foreign direct investment (FDI) is important for analyzing capital flows and the industrial organization of multinational firms. Most empirical studies of FDI, however, have focused on case studies of nontax factors in overseas investment decisions or on discerning simple correlations between some measure of direct investment and variables relating to nontax and tax aspects of the investment decision. These studies have helped to assess the qualitative effects of changes in the underlying determinants on firms' investment activities. It is more difficult to use those results for policy analysis. Our interest in investigating more precisely the links between tax policy parameters and investment stems from a concern that policymakers' consideration requires a richer empirical analysis.

At one level, this is a simple task. In theoretical studies, a number of authors have related tax parameters in "home" (residence) and "host" (source) countries to financial variables such as the cost of capital or the ratio of the market value of the firm to the replacement value of its capital stock.[1] Given such a relationship, one could apply familiar neoclassical investment models developed to explain firms' domestic investment decisions to estimate effects of tax parameters on outbound or inbound FDI.

Jason G. Cummins is assistant professor of economics at New York University and John M. Olin Fellow at Columbia University. R. Glenn Hubbard is the Russell L. Carson Professor of Economics and Finance at the Graduate School of Business of Columbia University and a research associate of the National Bureau of Economic Research.

Cummins thanks the Center for International Business Education and Research and the Chazen Institute at Columbia University for financial support. Hubbard acknowledges support from the Federal Reserve Bank of New York and a grant from the John M. Olin Foundation to the Center for the Study of the Economy and the State at the University of Chicago.

1. See, for example, Alworth 1988.

In practice, this exercise is far from simple. Studies of effects of tax parameters on (generally inbound) U.S. FDI rely on investment flows calculated by the Commerce Department's Bureau of Economic Analysis. These data do not distinguish between new capital investment and acquisitions of existing assets. Given our interest in the effects of tax policy on FDI, this definitional problem is potentially serious.[2]

We are able to mitigate this problem and apply familiar investment models by using previously unexplored (for this purpose) panel data on outbound FDI by individual subsidiaries of U.S. multinational firms, collected by Compustat's Geographic Segment file project.[3] These firm-level data contain information on new capital investment overseas, enabling us to measure tax influences on FDI more precisely and allowing us to focus on specific models of subsidiaries' new investment decisions. These models yield measures of the sensitivity of FDI to home- and host-country tax parameters.

8.2 Some Background on Empirical Studies

Existing empirical studies of FDI reflect researchers' interest in industrial organization or taxation. Industrial organization inquiries have generally ignored tax considerations and analyzed FDI as being governed by firms' desire to exploit the value of ownership-specific assets (such as valuable intangibles) or location-specific advantages (related to sourcing or marketing). Empirical research has analyzed the roles played by ownership-specific and location-specific variables in determining FDI. Public finance inquiries have focused on the role of differential tax treatment as determining the source and location of FDI, holding constant nontax determinants.[4]

In this vein, a significant body of empirical research has emphasized effects of taxation on inbound FDI in the United States. This literature has generally examined simple relationships between capital flows and measures of after-tax rates of return or effective tax rates on capital income.

Following work by Hartman (1984), several studies have used annual aggregate data for inbound FDI financed by subsidiary earnings and parent-company transfers of funds. Hartman's approach assumes that subsidiaries' dividend payouts are a residual in firm decisions. Payout ratios do not affect firms' required rate of return on equity invested, and permanent changes in home-country tax rates do not affect dividend payouts or the cost of capital. In the context of FDI, these implications permit Hartman and others to ignore effects of (at least permanent changes in) home-country tax parame-

---

2. In particular, Auerbach and Hassett (1993) have noted that neglecting the different tax treatments of the two forms of U.S. inbound FDI can lead to misleading results.
3. See Cummins and Hubbard 1995 for a discussion.
4. We review studies in both lines of inquiry in Cummins and Hubbard 1995.

ters on FDI in "mature" subsidiaries—that is, those paying dividends to their parent firms.[5]

Hartman estimates the effects on U.S. inbound FDI of changes in the after-tax rates of return received by foreign investors and by investors in U.S. capital generally, with the intent of measuring impacts of shifts in returns to new FDI. He finds that the FDI-GNP ratio increases as after-tax rates of return rise, and decreases as the relative tax rate on foreigners rises. These suggestive results indicate that taxes are an important determinant of FDI, and Hartman's study provoked many subsequent rounds of replication and refinement.[6]

Such studies are important advances on our understanding of the effects of taxation on FDI. A number of concerns arise, however. An obvious one relates to problems of inference about tax effects on *firms'* decisions using such highly aggregated data. Second, nontax determinants of FDI are not modeled. Finally, the "foreign direct investment" data supplied by the Bureau of Economic Analysis suffer two drawbacks, even accepting their level of aggregation: (1) they measure financial flows rather than new capital investment *per se;* and (2) they are based on periodic benchmark surveys, raising the possibility that FDI flows are more mismeasured the further the observation is from a benchmark year.

8.3   Using Firm-Level Data to Study FDI

8.3.1   Modeling Effects of Tax Parameters on FDI

In a world of ideal data, assessing the impact of taxation on firms' FDI decisions would be straightforward. Consider a U.S. parent firm deciding how much investment to pursue in a particular period. Intuitively, textbook neoclassical models of investment predict that the firm will invest until the value of an additional dollar of capital equals the cost of investing that dollar.

Unfortunately, this benchmark approach is not particularly useful as a practical guide to estimate effects of taxation on the levels of firms' FDI. First, it is difficult to develop a proxy for the incremental value of investing from available data on financial market valuation, even under the best of circumstances. For FDI, a further complication arises because location-specific effects on the value of incremental investment in the subsidiary cannot be captured by using available financial data at the parent-firm level, and subsidiary-specific financial market data are, of course, not generally available.

To reduce these practical problems, we employ an empirical approach devel-

5. This approach is more suitably applied to firm-level data. The underlying model suggests that a mature subsidiary's investment financed by retained earnings is unaffected by the home-country tax rate. This suggestion is not equivalent to a claim that *aggregate* investment out of retained earnings will not be affected by the home-country tax rate.

6. See, for example, Boskin and Gale 1987; Newlon 1987; Slemrod 1990.

oped to estimate effects on investment of after-tax returns to investing with fewer informational requirements than in conventional models.[7] Nonetheless, the approach still allows us to ask, given a change in a tax parameter, how does a subsidiary's return on additional investment change, and how does FDI change in response?

Tax considerations can affect subsidiaries' new capital investment decisions through two channels.[8] First, host-country corporate income tax rates, investment incentives, and depreciation rules affect the cost of capital for foreign investors. This channel has been the focus of empirical analysis of effects of tax policy on domestic investment.

A second channel through which tax policy affects FDI from countries with worldwide tax systems[9] such as the United States is through variation over time and across firms in the "tax price" of subsidiaries' dividend repatriations to their parent firms. Within our approach, subsidiary dividend decisions and the cost of capital are not affected by permanent changes in the tax price of repatriations, though temporary changes can affect both repatriations and FDI.[10]

There are two sources of variation in the tax price of dividend repatriations. The first reflects variation over time in host- and home-country statutory corporate income tax rates. The second reflects variation in foreign tax credit status (that is, excess credit or excess limit positions) both across firms and over time for a given firm. Parents in an excess limit position owe residual U.S. corporate tax if the U.S. corporate tax rate exceeds the applicable foreign tax rate. Parents in an excess credit position owe no residual U.S. corporate tax.

Our empirical tests analyze effects of changes in pretax returns to investing and in the tax parameters described above on FDI by U.S. multinational firms. Execution of these tests requires firm-level data on multinationals and their subsidiaries; we describe these data briefly below.

7. For a technical description, see Cummins and Hubbard 1995.

8. A different set of tax determinants is in general relevant for investment through acquisitions. See, for example, the discussion in Auerbach and Hassett 1993.

9. By worldwide tax system, we mean that the home country taxes the worldwide income of multinational firms (generally when repatriated), but grants a foreign tax credit (subject to limitation).

10. That is, we work within a framework known as the "trapped-equity" or "tax-capitalization" view of corporate dividends. A simple example illustrates this view. Suppose that a parent firm capitalizes a wholly owned subsidiary with an initial transfer of equity capital. When the subsidiary has growth opportunities and desired investment exceeds internally generated funds, the parent transfers additional funds to it. For a mature subsidiary, equity is "trapped"—earnings exceed profitable investment opportunities, and the subsidiary repatriates the residual funds. Costly repatriation can be delayed so long as the subsidiary has active investment opportunities abroad, but once those are exhausted, the subpart F rules prevent the use of passive investments to defer U.S. tax obligations. In this trapped-equity view, subsidiary dividend payouts are unaffected by permanent changes in their tax price. While this view is controversial in the context of dividend payouts from a domestic firm to its shareholders (owing to potential information or corporate control problems), it is arguably less controversial in our application to dividends paid by majority- or wholly-owned subsidiaries to their parent firms.

Table 8.1   **Number of U.S. Foreign Subsidiaries in Sample**

Year	Canada	United Kingdom	Germany	France	Japan	Australia	Total
1980	225	25	12	3	4	13	282
1981	224	36	12	4	5	12	293
1982	242	45	11	5	7	14	324
1983	254	54	10	5	10	13	346
1984	272	58	13	6	15	14	378
1985	307	81	16	10	19	18	451
1986	320	94	19	11	23	24	491
1987	346	105	22	11	26	23	533
1988	362	104	21	11	24	24	546
1989	394	113	20	11	25	26	589
1990	403	121	32	15	29	32	632
1991	366	119	29	17	25	26	582

Source: Authors' calculations.

8.3.2   Constructing Firm-Level Data on FDI

The data set is constructed from the Compustat Geographic Segment file.[11] Approximately 6,500 companies report information from their foreign operations, segregated by geographic segment. Both U.S.- and foreign-incorporated firms report sales, operating income, and fixed assets. Up to four geographic regions are reported for seven years at a time. We combine two seven-year panels to obtain a data set on outbound FDI by U.S. multinational corporations over the period 1980 to 1991.

Table 8.1 indicates the number of U.S. foreign subsidiaries reporting information in the Compustat data. Countries for which Compustat reports data are Canada, the United Kingdom, (the former West) Germany, France, Japan, and Australia. While the number of subsidiaries reporting information varies from year to year (generally growing over the period), we are able to obtain investment and operating information on between 282 and 632 U.S. foreign subsidiaries.

8.3.3   Estimating Effects of Tax Parameters on FDI

In Cummins and Hubbard 1995, we estimated a model of investment by subsidiaries of U.S. multinationals that is derived from recent studies of determinants of domestic business fixed investment. Using the panel data described

---

11. Geographic segment disclosures are mandated by *Statement of Financial Accounting Standards No. 14: Financial Reporting of Segments in a Business Enterprise* (*SFAS 14*), issued in 1976. *SFAS 14* was designed to provide information useful for evaluating the nature of the firm's investment and production decisions. *SFAS 14* requires firms to disclose information about foreign sales, income, and fixed assets if foreign operations account for at least 10 percent of a firm's revenue or assets.

above on investment by U.S. subsidiaries in Canada, the United Kingdom, Germany, France, Australia, and Japan, we tested the hypothesis that host- and home-country tax parameters should be included in the model, and estimated the responsiveness of subsidiary investment to pretax returns and tax parameters.

Our results can be described straightforwardly in two steps. First, we reject conclusively the simple notion that "taxes don't matter"—both host- and home-country tax parameters should be included in the correct specification of the subsidiary's investment model. Second, we estimate a significant responsiveness of firm-level FDI to the tax-adjusted cost of capital. Our results suggest that each percentage-point increase in the cost of capital leads to a 1–2 percentage-point decrease in the annual rate of investment (investment divided by the beginning-of-period capital stock).[12] Changes in the cost of capital can reflect, among other things, the host- and home-country tax variables we discussed in section 8.3.1.

Our findings are consistent with the hypothesis that permanent changes in the tax price of subsidiary dividend repatriations do not affect the cost of capital or FDI by dividend-paying subsidiaries. This result allows us to offer some observations about the extent to which the U.S. system of taxing multinationals' income corresponds to norms of capital-export neutrality or capital-import neutrality.[13] Hartman (1984) and others have noted that, for dividend-paying subsidiaries, permanent changes in the home-country (U.S.) corporate tax rate should have no effect on FDI financed out of subsidiary retained earnings—a "capital-import neutral" result for these firms. This finding does not carry over precisely in our framework, since changes in the parent firm's foreign tax credit status also affect the tax price of repatriations. Hence, Hartman's result holds in the case for which the parent's foreign tax credit position is not expected to change. With expected changes in foreign tax credit status, capital-export neutrality may prevail. Similar examples can be constructed for "immature" subsidiaries, those financing initial investment using parent equity transfers.[14] To summarize, the U.S. tax system creates potentially complex effects of tax parameters on overseas investment decisions, and those effects can vary significantly across firms.

12. These estimates are broadly consistent with those reported for firm-level fixed investment in the United States (see Cummins, Hassett, and Hubbard, 1994a) and with those for firm-level domestic fixed investment in other OECD countries (see Cummins, Harris, and Hassett, 1995; Cummins, Hassett, and Hubbard 1994b).

13. Capital-export neutrality results when the home country's tax parameters do not distort a domestic investor's decision between investing at home or abroad. Capital-import neutrality results when domestic and foreign investments in a country have equivalent overall investor tax treatment. In practice, no industrialized country's tax system corresponds precisely to the norms of capital-export neutrality or capital-import neutrality. The U.S. Treasury has generally argued for capital-export-neutral policy benchmark, though the U.S. system's allowance for deferral of tax on overseas profits until repatriated (among other considerations) is inconsistent with capital-export neutrality.

14. We review such examples in detail in Cummins and Hubbard 1995.

8.4   Conclusions and Directions for Future Research

Our study represents a first step in a research program to use microdata on multinational firms' overseas investment decisions to study the determinants of FDI, especially those related to tax policy. The panel data that we use on FDI of subsidiaries of U.S. firms permit us to focus on "new investment," a focus not possible with studies that use aggregate data. These data allow us to test models of investment decisions that yield informative estimates of effects of tax parameters on FDI.

We believe we have been successful in two respects. First, we have extended conventional investment models to accommodate a wide range of tax influences on FDI decisions. Second, our empirical results cast significant doubt on the simple notion that taxes don't matter for U.S. firms' FDI decisions. Indeed, tax parameters influence FDI in precisely the ways indicated by standard models of investment.

We are pursuing three extensions. First, we are adapting our analysis to study effects of tax policy on FDI in the United States by foreign firms. Second, we plan to examine whether, as a result of exchange rate shifts, revaluations of firms' profits in terms of host-country currency affect their FDI. Finally, we will incorporate imperfect competition and intangible assets more explicitly in our approach.

References

Alworth, Julian S. 1988. *The finance, investment, and taxation decisions of multinationals.* Oxford: Basil Blackwell.

Altshuler, Rosanne, and T. Scott Newlon. 1993. The effects of U.S. tax policy on the income repatriation patterns of U.S. multinational corporations. In *Studies in international taxation,* ed. Alberto Giovannini, R. Glenn Hubbard, and Joel Slemrod. Chicago: University of Chicago Press.

Altshuler, Rosanne, T. Scott Newlon, and William C. Randolph. 1995. Tax effects on income repatriation by U.S. multinationals: Evidence from panel data. In *The effects of taxation on multinational corporations,* ed. Martin Feldstein, James R. Hines, Jr., and R. Glenn Hubbard. Chicago: University of Chicago Press.

Auerbach, Alan J., and Kevin A. Hassett. 1993. Taxation and foreign direct investment in the United States: A reconsideration of the evidence. In *Studies in international taxation,* ed. Alberto Giovannini, R. Glenn Hubbard, and Joel B. Slemrod. Chicago: University of Chicago Press.

Boskin, Michael J., and William G. Gale. 1987. New results on the effects of tax policy on the international location of investment. In *The effects of taxation on capital accumulation,* ed. Martin Feldstein. Chicago: University of Chicago Press.

Cummins, Jason G., Trevor S. Harris, and Kevin A. Hassett. 1995. Accounting standards, information flow, and firm investment behavior. In *The effects of taxation on multinational corporations,* ed. Martin Feldstein, James R. Hines, Jr., and R. Glenn Hubbard. Chicago: University of Chicago Press.

Cummins, Jason G., Kevin A. Hassett, and R. Glenn Hubbard. 1994a. A reconsideration of investment behavior using tax reforms as natural experiments. *Brookings Papers on Economic Activity* 1994:2.

———. 1994b. Using tax reforms to study investment decisions: An international study. Columbia University. Mimeo.

Cummins, Jason G., and R. Glenn Hubbard. 1995. The tax sensitivity of foreign direct investment: Evidence from firm-level panel data. In *The effects of taxation on multinational corporations,* ed. Martin Feldstein, James R. Hines, Jr., and R. Glenn Hubbard. Chicago: University of Chicago Press.

Hartman, David G. 1984. Tax policy and foreign direct investment in the United States. *National Tax Journal* 37 (December): 475–87.

Hines, James R., Jr., and R. Glenn Hubbard. 1990. Coming home to America: Dividend repatriations by U.S. multinationals. In *Taxation in the global economy,* ed. Assaf Razin and Joel B. Slemrod. Chicago: University of Chicago Press.

Newlon, T. Scott. 1987. Tax policy and the multinational firm's financial policy and investment decisions. Ph.D. dissertation, Princeton University.

Slemrod, Joel B. 1990. Tax effects on foreign direct investment in the United States: Evidence from a cross-country comparison. In *Taxation in the global economy,* ed. Assaf Razin and Joel Slemrod. Chicago: University of Chicago Press.

9   The Tax Treatment of Interest and the Operations of U.S. Multinationals

Kenneth A. Froot and James R. Hines, Jr.

9.1   Introduction

The taxation of multinational corporations entails a number of complications beyond those that accompany ordinary business taxation. One of the most complex and important aspects of taxing multinational firms is the treatment of interest expenses. Multinational firms may borrow money in one country in order to deploy the funds elsewhere. Firms are entitled to claim tax deductions for their interest costs, but the countries in which they borrow may not permit all of the associated interest expenses to be deducted against local income for tax purposes. The method used to calculate allowable interest tax deductions can, in turn, affect financing choices and operating decisions.

American tax law permits only partial deductibility of the interest expenses of multinational firms. U.S. law specifies rules that determine the extent to which interest costs incurred by multinational firms in the United States can be deducted for tax purposes against U.S. income. These rules are often changed, the last major change occurring in 1986.

This paper describes the impact on firm behavior of the change in the U.S. interest allocation rules introduced by the Tax Reform Act of 1986. The act significantly reduced the tax deductibility of the U.S. interest expenses of certain American multinational corporations. Congress changed the law in 1986

Kenneth A. Froot is professor of business administration at Harvard Business School and a research associate of the National Bureau of Economic Research. James R. Hines, Jr., is associate professor of public policy at the John F. Kennedy School of Government of Harvard University and a faculty research fellow of the National Bureau of Economic Research.

The authors are grateful to Paul O'Connell for outstanding research assistance, and to Julie Collins for helpful comments on an earlier draft. Generous research support was provided by NBER, the Division of Research at Harvard Business School, and the National Science Foundation (grant SES-9209373).

because it was concerned that U.S.-based firms received tax deductions for interest expenses on borrowing undertaken in the United States to enhance their profits overseas. The act introduced a new formula for multinational firms to use in calculating the fraction of their interest expenses that can be deducted against taxable income in the United States.

This tax change increased the tax liabilities of certain American multinationals, and made additional borrowing more expensive for these firms. One of the concerns raised during the deliberations over the act was that this additional cost of borrowing might discourage some firms from investing in new plant and equipment, since a sizable fraction of new investment is financed by borrowing. The object of this paper is to examine the impact of the tax change on the operations of those multinational firms that were affected by the change in interest allocation rules. To do so, it is necessary to compare the behavior of the affected firms to the behavior of those firms that were unaffected by the interest allocation provisions of the 1986 act.

The results indicate that the change in interest allocation rules significantly influenced the operations of American multinational firms. Firms that were unable to deduct all of their interest expenses against their U.S. tax liabilities issued 4.2 percent less debt between 1986 and 1991 (measured as a fraction of total firm assets), and invested 3.5 percent less in property, plant, and equipment, than did other firms. In addition, the affected firms showed a greater proclivity to lease rather than own capital assets, and to reduce the scope of their foreign operations. All of these behavioral responses are consistent with the incentives created by the interest allocation provisions of the Tax Reform Act of 1986.

Section 9.2 describes the U.S. tax treatment of the interest expenses of multinational corporations, and analyzes the incentives created by the Tax Reform Act of 1986. Section 9.3 describes the data used to analyze the impact of the 1986 tax change, and presents the results of regressions that estimate the impact of the tax change on various aspects of the operations of American multinational firms. Section 9.4 is the conclusion.

9.2   The Tax Treatment of Interest Expense

This section identifies the incentives created by the Tax Reform Act of 1986, in order to facilitate the analysis of the impact of the act on the behavior of U.S. firms.

Interest expenses are generally deductible against the taxable income of U.S. corporations. There are, however, two important circumstances in which the deductibility of interest is of limited value to an interest-paying corporation. The first arises when a corporation has negative profits before interest deductions. Since a firm with losses pays no taxes, interest deductions do not reduce its tax liability. Corporations are permitted, however, to carry net operating losses backward up to three years or forward up to fifteen years.[1] The second circumstance is one in which a firm is subject to the corporate alternative minimum tax (AMT); firms paying the AMT face idiosyncratic tax incentives.[2]

9.2.1 Foreign and Domestic Allocation of Interest Deductions

Special problems arise in allocating the interest deductions of multinational firms. The idea that underlies U.S. law is that, when a multinational firm incurs interest expense in the United States, a certain fraction of the expense should be allocated as a deduction against taxable domestic income, and the remainder allocated against the firm's foreign income. The respective fractions are determined on the basis of the income-generating capacity created by the loans on which interest is paid. The extreme difficulty that this concept encounters is that it is not always clear to what extent a particular loan generates domestic-source and foreign-source income.

In order to understand the significance of the sourcing of interest deductions, it is necessary to consider the treatment of foreign-source income. The appendix to this volume describes the U.S. tax treatment of income earned by multinational corporations. Due to some peculiarities of the changes in U.S. tax law after 1986, certain firms found that the cost of debt changed significantly between 1986 and 1987. The goal of the empirical work described in section 9.3 is to follow and compare the behavior of those firms facing higher costs of debt to those firms facing unchanged cost of debt.

9.2.2 Interaction of Interest Expense and Foreign Income Rules

American firms with foreign income are generally not permitted to deduct all of their interest costs in the United States against their domestic taxable incomes. Instead, the law provides for various methods of allocating interest expenses between domestic and foreign income. The intent of the law is to retain the full deductibility of interest expense against taxable U.S. income, but only for that part of interest expense generating income that is subject to U.S. taxation.

From the standpoint of taxpaying firms, the U.S. tax law's distinction between domestic and foreign interest deductions is potentially quite important. If interest expense is deemed to be domestic, then it is deductible against the taxpayer's U.S. taxable income. If it is deemed to be foreign, then the interest expense reduces foreign taxable income *for the purposes of U.S. income taxa-*

---

1. Tax-loss carryforwards do not accrue interest, a feature that limits their value even to firms that expect to have taxable profits in the future. Scholes and Wolfson (1992) analyze the value of tax-loss carryforwards in uncertain environments.

2. For the remainder of the paper, we analyze taxpaying firms that are not subject to the AMT. Lyon and Silverstein (1995) report that 30.7 percent of firms with assets over $500 million paid the AMT in 1990.

tion only. Foreign governments do not use U.S. methods of calculating interest deductions and generally do not permit U.S. firms to reduce their taxable incomes in foreign countries on the basis of interest expenses incurred in the United States. Consequently, interest expenses allocated against foreign income are valuable to a U.S. firm only if it has deficit foreign tax credits. If it does have deficit credits, then some of the firm's foreign income is subject to U.S. tax, and any additional dollar of interest expense allocated against foreign income reduces the firm's U.S. taxable income by a dollar.[3] With deficit foreign tax credits, firms are indifferent between allocating interest expenses against foreign income and allocating them against domestic income.[4] If, on the other hand, firms have excess foreign tax credits, then any interest expenses allocated against foreign income are useless from the standpoint of reducing tax liabilities, since foreign income generates no U.S. tax liability anyway.

The Tax Reform Act of 1986 significantly changed U.S. tax law governing the allocation of interest expenses. Prior to 1986, the interest expenses of U.S. taxpayers were determined separately for each company within a controlled group.[5] In principle, each company was required to allocate interest deductions between domestic and foreign source in proportion to domestic and foreign assets.[6] In practice, however, this rule permitted taxpayers to structure their finances in order to obtain a full tax deduction in the United States for interest expenses associated with borrowing done in the United States.

Consider, for example, the situation of an American corporation that borrows $100 in the United States, paying interest of $10 annually. The corporation has $150 of U.S. assets and $50 of foreign assets, and earns profits of

3. Curiously, the law is written so that the additional dollar of interest expense reduces taxable income without reducing the foreign tax credits available for foreign income taxes paid.

4. This statement, along with much of the analysis described in the paper, abstracts from the ability of firms to carry excess foreign tax credits backward two years and forward five years. Firms that carry excess credits forward or back may (depending on specific circumstances) face incentives that are intermediate between those of deficit credit and excess credit firms.

5. Separate allocation of interest deductions for each company within a controlled group was firmly established by Treasury Regulation section 1.861-8, issued in 1977. Prior to 1977, U.S. law was somewhat vague about whether all of the companies within a controlled group should be consolidated for purposes of interest allocation, though in an important case based on pre-1977 law (*ITT v. United States*), the courts held that interest should be allocated on a consolidated basis.

6. Taxpayers were given the alternative of allocating interest deductions on the basis of gross domestic income and gross foreign income, though it is hard to understand why a tax-minimizing corporation would do so, since tax-planning opportunities are so attractive using the asset method on a single-company basis. The regulation provides that, if the income method is chosen, interest deductions allocated against foreign-source income cannot be less than 50 percent of the amount that would have been allocated against foreign-source income by the asset method. Taxpayers allocating their interest deductions on the basis of domestic and foreign assets were required to do so based on the book values of those assets, unless the taxpayer elected to allocate on the basis of fair market values, and could demonstrate fair market values to the satisfaction of the IRS. Once chosen, taxpayers were required to continue to use the fair market value method until granted permission by the IRS to discontinue its use. Book values of stock (such as parent corporation's stock in its foreign subsidiaries) were not adjusted to include undistributed earnings and profits reinvested by the subsidiary corporations.

$15, gross of interest costs, in the United States, and profits of $5 abroad. The corporation does no foreign borrowing. Under pre-1986 law, this corporation would be entitled to deduct only $7.50 (75 percent of $10) of its interest charges against U.S. income, since only 75 percent of its assets produce U.S.-source income; the remaining $2.50 of interest deductions would be allocated against foreign-source income. The same firm, with the same real business activities, could, however, reorganize its affairs in a manner that would permit all of the $10 interest cost to be deductible against U.S. income. To do so, the parent firm need only borrow the $100 in the U.S. market and then contribute the money as paid-in capital to a wholly owned domestic subsidiary that owns the firm's domestic and foreign operations. The domestic subsidiary pays all of its profits to its parent as dividends. The parent firm and the domestic subsidiary file a consolidated tax return and annual report. The domestic subsidiary has $15 of U.S.-source income and $5 of foreign-source income; it has no interest expenses. The parent firm has $20 of income on the basis of dividends received from its subsidiary, and $10 of interest deductions. The parent firm is entitled to deduct all of its interest expense against U.S. income, since the firm's assets (its wholly owned subsidiary) are all in the United States.[7]

The Tax Reform Act of 1986 significantly changed the method by which interest deductions are allocated, specifically by introducing a "one-taxpayer rule" in which the attributes of all members of a controlled group—whether owned directly by a parent firm or owned by the parent through one or more subsidiaries—determine the allocation of interest deductions between domestic and foreign income.[8] The motivation for the tax change was the insight that financial fungibility implies that borrowing by one part of a controlled group directly or indirectly influences the economic activities of all of the group. The act provides that the interest expenses of a U.S. taxpayer should be allocated between domestic-source and foreign-source income based on the relative assets of the domestic and foreign operations of the controlled group. Of course, several complications attend the implementation of such a rule.

Taxpayers are required to allocate interest deductions between domestic and foreign source on the basis of the book values of assets held domestically and abroad.[9] In the cases of subsidiaries that are 10 percent or more owned by members of the affiliated group, the book values of stock held in the sub-

---

7. Prior to 1986, U.S. law did not use sophisticated "look-through" rules to determine the extent to which a U.S. corporation represents a U.S. asset. Instead, a U.S.-located subsidiary was considered to be a U.S. asset as long as 20 percent or more of its gross income for the prior three years had U.S. source. In the example, 75 percent of the domestic subsidiary's gross income has U.S. source.

8. The changes in the interest allocation rules introduced by the Tax Reform Act of 1986 were phased in over three years. Various phase-in rules apply to the interest on debt issued between 1983 and 1985.

9. Taxpayers have the alternative of using the fair market values of assets held domestically and abroad, but if taxpayers do so, they are not again able to use book values without permission of the IRS.

sidiaries are adjusted to reflect accumulated earnings and profits of the subsidiaries. Hence, in the case of an American firm that initially finances its wholly owned French subsidiary with $100 of equity, and in which the subsidiary subsequently earns and reinvests an additional $400, the parent's book value of the subsidiary is adjusted to $500 for purposes of interest expense allocation.

The 1986 act provides for a curious treatment of foreign assets and foreign interest deductions by members of a controlled group. For this purpose, the gross value of U.S. assets and the net value of foreign assets are used. This leads to a somewhat asymmetric treatment of foreign and domestic borrowing for purposes of interest expense allocation. Consider, for example, the case of a U.S. firm that has $200 of U.S. assets, of which $150 is equity and $50 is debt borrowed from an unrelated party; the firm also has $200 of foreign assets, of which $150 is parent equity and $50 is debt borrowed by the subsidiary from an unrelated foreign party. The firm has U.S.-source gross income of $40, U.S. interest cost of $5, foreign-source gross income of $40, and foreign-source interest expense of $5. This firm is required to allocate almost half of its $5 domestic interest deduction against foreign-source income,[10] and the firm is not permitted to allocate any of its foreign interest expense against domestic-source income, even though the leverage situation of the foreign subsidiary is the same as the leverage situation of its American parent.

One of the consequences of the asymmetric treatment of U.S. parent firms and their foreign subsidiaries is that the tax law can encourage firms to finance their subsidiaries with debt from the American parent instead of parent equity or unrelated-party debt. Parent equity in foreign subsidiaries reduces the amount of domestic interest payments allocated against U.S.-source income. If, in the previous example, the subsidiary borrowed $50 from its parent company instead of from an unrelated party, and the parent financed the loan to its subsidiary by borrowing an additional $50 from unrelated U.S. parties, then the subsidiary's tax position would not change (it still gets a $5 deduction against taxable income in the foreign country for interest paid to its U.S. parent),[11] but the parent firm would receive a larger interest deduction against U.S.-source income. The U.S. Treasury issued regulations designed to prevent U.S. firms from reacting to the passage of the 1986 act by financing their foreign subsidiaries with loans from U.S. parents financed by U.S. borrowing.[12]

10. The firm has domestic assets of $200 and foreign book assets of $150, so it allocates four-sevenths ($200/$350) of its domestic interest expense against domestic-source income, and the remaining three-sevenths against foreign-source income.

11. Subject to two qualifications. Certain countries (including the United States) impose "thin-capitalization" laws that limit the amount of related-party interest foreign firms can deduct from local taxable income. In addition, countries often impose withholding taxes on cross-border interest payments; U.S. firms with deficit foreign tax credits receive foreign tax credits for paying these taxes. Withholding taxes on interest are usually reduced, often to zero, by bilateral tax treaties.

12. Details of these regulations are described in Froot and Hines 1995.

9.2.3   Incentives Created by the Tax Rules

The upshot of the rules just described is that firms with excess foreign tax credits and substantial foreign assets (as a fraction of total assets) could no longer enjoy the benefits of full deductibility of interest expenses incurred in the United States after 1986. Firms with deficit foreign tax credits, or those with no foreign assets, retain full benefits of interest expense deductibility. As a consequence, firms in the first category can be expected to reduce their borrowing relative to firms in the second, and can also be expected to reduce the volume of their debt-financed investment activity.[13]

9.3   Data and Results

This section describes the data used to analyze firm reactions to the Tax Reform Act of 1986. The section presents the details of the procedure used to construct our sample of firms and some statistics that describe aspects of the behavior of these firms after 1986.

9.3.1   The Sample

We use information reported by Compustat on the balance-sheet items of large publicly traded corporations. Compustat currently provides information on more than 7,500 companies. We select only multinational firms incorporated in the United States: firms are included if their reported foreign assets equal 1 percent or more of reported total assets for *each* year during 1986–90. Four hundred twenty-two firms satisfy this criterion.

Foreign tax rate information is central to our analysis, since the hypothesis that firms maximize after-tax profits implies that deficit foreign tax credit firms will react quite differently to the Tax Reform Act of 1986 than will excess foreign tax credit firms. We construct foreign tax rates as the ratio of foreign income taxes paid to foreign pretax income as reported by Compustat. This variable is somewhat noisy, but is likely to capture the major differences between the foreign tax rates facing different firms.[14] In order to attenuate some

---

13. Two other studies examine the impact of interest allocation rules on the behavior of impacted firms. Collins and Shackelford (1992) find that firms with large ratios of foreign to domestic assets are more likely than other firms to issue preferred stock (as a substitute for debt) in the period after 1986. Collins and Shackelford do not, however, distinguish excess foreign tax credit firms from deficit foreign tax credit firms. Altshuler and Mintz (1994) analyze the borrowing patterns of a sample of eight multinational firms, finding that firms that are unable to claim full tax deductions for interest payments in the United States are more likely to borrow abroad than to borrow in the United States.

14. The introduction of the new interest allocation rules in 1986, along with other tax changes, gave some firms incentives to adjust the location and tax-avoiding behavior of their foreign affiliates. In the analysis that follows, we take foreign tax rates to be exogenous to U.S. tax changes. Endogenizing foreign tax rates could change the interpretation of the magnitude of the estimated effects.

of the difficulties that accompany annual measurements of the foreign tax rate variable, firms are classified into excess foreign tax credit status based on five years of data, 1986–90. Firms for which the average foreign tax rate over that period exceeds the contemporaneous average U.S. statutory corporate tax rate are classified as excess foreign tax credit firms; all other firms are classified as deficit foreign tax credit firms.[15] From our initial sample of 422 firms, six additional firms are excluded, five due to insufficient tax rate information, and one to major ownership changes over the 1986–91 period.

Firms that merge or acquire new firms may face dramatic changes in their tax business environments that have the potential to confound the analysis of their tax-motivated behavior. In some of the statistical work that follows, we exclude firms that show changes in total assets of 100 percent or more in single years, doing so with the idea of excluding firms involved in major mergers or acquisitions. This restriction reduces the sample size to 388 firms. Froot and Hines 1995 provides additional description of the sample of its construction.

We measure changes in debt as the difference between total debt (long-term and current) in 1991 and total debt in 1986. Changes in capital are measured as the difference between net property, plant, and equipment in 1991 and that in 1986. Foreign assets are measured as total foreign assets in 1986, and the ratio of this variable to total assets in 1986 is used not only to control for firm characteristics (degree of multinationality) but as part of the cost of debt finance after 1986.[16]

9.3.2   Behavior of the Sample

Table 9.1 describes the behavior of our sample of firms after 1986. Firms are classified into two groups on the basis of fraction of foreign assets (above median and below median); within group, they are further classified by excess foreign tax credit and deficit foreign tax credit status. Roughly half of the firms in the sample (51.4 percent) are classified as having excess foreign tax credits.

Firms that differ in the fraction of their assets held abroad are likely to differ in other important observable and unobservable ways. The after-tax cost of debt-financed investments rose most sharply after 1986 for firms with excess foreign tax credits and significant foreign assets. The behavior described in table 9.1 is consistent with predicted patterns. Firms with excess foreign tax credits exhibit slower mean growth (from 1986 to 1991) of outstanding debt

---

15. This classification of the foreign tax credit status of the firms in the sample is necessarily somewhat imprecise. The same firm may have excess foreign tax credits in one year and deficit foreign tax credits in another; furthermore, excess foreign tax credits may be carried forward five years or back two years. A firm's foreign tax credit status can be endogenous to discretionary decisions such as dividend repatriation choices. Experimentation with other methods of distinguishing excess foreign tax credit firms from deficit foreign tax credit firms had little impact on the results.

16. The mean ratio of foreign to total assets in our sample for 1986 is 0.247; the median is 0.219, and the standard deviation is 0.152.

Table 9.1   **Debt and Property, Plant, and Equipment Accumulation, by Foreign Asset Concentration and Foreign Tax Credit Status, 1986–1991**

	Foreign Assets/Total Assets below Median		Foreign Assets/Total Assets above Median	
	Excess FTC	Deficit FTC	Excess FTC	Deficit FTC
Number of firms	97	96	92	101
(Change in debt)/assets				
Mean	0.13678	0.13426	0.10556	0.15447
Median	0.11705	0.05519	0.06016	0.14446
Standard deviation	0.28151	0.22383	0.12348	0.24886
(Change in PPE)/assets				
Mean	0.13847	0.15538	0.13395	0.18940
Median	0.11121	0.07145	0.13104	0.14902
Standard deviation	0.24350	0.29645	0.22000	0.29366

Notes: Firms are classified into cells based on foreign assets/total assets ratios in 1986, and by foreign tax credit (FTC) status as calculated over the 1986–91 period. (Change in debt)/assets is the difference between total debt in 1991 and total debt in 1986, divided by total assets in 1986. (Change in PPE)/assets is the difference between net property, plant, and equipment in 1991 and net property, plant, and equipment in 1986, divided by total assets in 1986.

relative to 1986 assets, and slower mean growth of property, plant, and equipment, than do deficit credit firms. This pattern appears for multinational firms with small fractions of foreign assets (except for a negligible difference in debt changes for excess and deficit foreign tax credit firms with small amounts of foreign assets), but is considerably more dramatic for firms with high fractions of foreign assets.

Figure 9.1 illustrates the mean growth of debt relative to 1986 asset levels for firms in each cell reported in table 9.1. The figure indicates that the impact of excess foreign tax credits appears only in firms with significant foreign assets, which is consistent with the discussion in section 9.2. Furthermore, there is a marked difference between the cumulative growth of debt in excess foreign tax credit firms and deficit foreign tax credit firms. A similar pattern appears in firms' accumulation of property, plant, and equipment, as illustrated by figure 9.2. This figure indicates that the impact of excess foreign tax credits on the accumulation of property, plant, and equipment is most dramatic for firms with significant foreign assets as a fraction of total assets.

Froot and Hines 1995 provides a more detailed statistical analysis of the behavior of the firms in this sample. The statistical results are quite consistent with the picture that emerges from table 9.1 and figures 9.1 and 9.2. Even after controlling for industry and degree of multinationality, firms that were unable to deduct 100 percent of their U.S. interest expenses accumulated 4.2 percent less debt (measured as a fraction of total firm assets) and 3.5 percent less property, plant, and equipment than did other firms over the period 1986–91.

There are two possible interpretations of the tendency for firms with excess

ΔDebt/1986 Assets

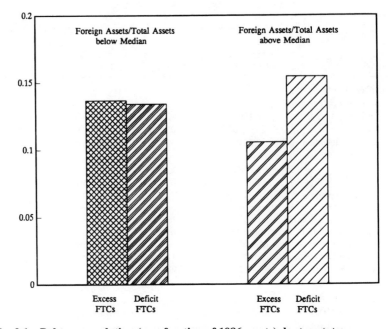

Fig. 9.1   Debt accumulation (as a fraction of 1986 assets), by tax status, 1986–1991

Notes: Bars measure the ratios of five-year changes (1986–91) in book values of debt to 1986 book assets. Entries depict this ratio for the firm with the median ratio in each characteristic. Of the 193 firms with below-median ratios of foreign assets to total assets in 1986, 97 were classified as having excess foreign tax credits and 96 as having deficit foreign tax credits. Of the 193 firms with above-median ratios of foreign assets to total assets, 92 were classified as having excess foreign tax credits and 101 as having deficit foreign tax credits.

foreign tax credits and high ratios of foreign to total assets to accumulate property, plant, and equipment more slowly than do other firms. The first is that the loss of debt tax shields experienced by these firms results in a higher overall cost of capital and, consequently, a lower level of investment. Of course, to the extent that firms substitute away from debt finance toward cheaper after-tax financing sources, these substitutions can mitigate the increased cost of capital.[17]

The second interpretation is that firms do not face *any* increases in the cost

---

17. In an extreme case, it is possible for these substitutions to reduce to zero the cost of the change in the interest allocation rules. The size of the predicted cost corresponds to the ease with which firms can adjust their financial and operating patterns. Naturally, different models of firm behavior carry different predictions. Stiglitz (1973) argues that the tax advantage to debt makes borrowing a firm's preferred method of financing marginal investments. If this argument is correct, and firms continue to prefer debt to other financing methods even after some of its tax advantages are lost due to the interest allocation rules, then firms will react to the tax changes, not by substitut-

ΔPPE/1986 Assets

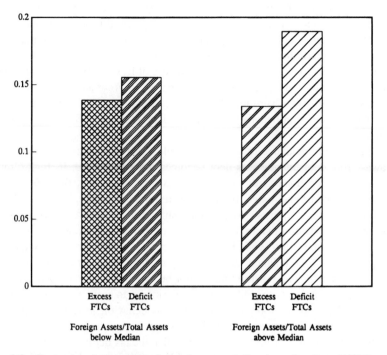

Fig. 9.2   Property, plant, and equipment accumulation (as a fraction of 1986 assets), by tax status, 1986–1991
Notes: Bars measure the ratios of five-year changes (1986–91) in book values of property, plant, and equipment (PPE) to 1986 book assets. Entries depict this ratio for the firm with the median ratio in each characteristic. Of the 193 firms with below-median ratios of foreign assets to total assets in 1986, 97 were classified as having excess foreign tax credits and 96 as having deficit foreign tax credits. Of the 193 firms with above-median ratios of foreign assets to total assets, 92 were classified as having excess foreign tax credits and 101 as having deficit foreign tax credits.

of *employing* capital, but that they reduce property, plant, and equipment expenditures by leasing rather than owning capital. Lease prices reflect both the costs of depreciation and the costs of holding capital. The tax law, however, entitles lessees to deduct the full costs of their lease payments, without allocating the capital component between foreign and domestic source. Hence, if a

---

ing other financing methods for debt, but by reducing the size of foreign and total operations. Alternatively, the Miller (1977) model of financial equilibrium implies that firms impacted by the interest allocation rules will change their capital structures to pure equity finance. As long as the capitalization of the affected firms does not exceed the initial amount of equity on the market, this type of financial arbitrage implies that the interest allocation rules will not affect the capital costs, or real operations, of any firms. Gordon and Malkiel (1981) examine a model in which debt is tax-preferred, but its use raises the probability that a firm will incur costs associated with bankruptcy; this model carries implications between those of the Stiglitz and Miller models.

multinational firm leases capital from a debt-financed, purely domestic entity, the interest cost of holding that capital will be fully deductible against U.S. taxes. Thus, leases may represent low-cost devices to preserve the tax shield for a given amount of property, plant, and equipment. This suggests that excess foreign tax credit firms—particularly those with higher foreign asset ratios—had incentives to expand more rapidly the use of leases than did deficit foreign tax credit firms. And indeed, evidence reported in Froot and Hines 1995 indicates that firms that were unable to deduct 100 percent of their U.S. interest expenses were significantly more likely than were other firms to undertake new leases after 1986.[18]

The leasing evidence raises the possibility that firms can easily substitute away from debt financing as debt becomes more expensive. If, for example, leasing can be done at the same after-tax cost as buying, then the tax-law change may just encourage low-cost substitution. Of course, it is unlikely that wholesale substitution is costless, and many of the results are also consistent with the proposition that excess foreign tax credit firms face relatively greater costs of capital after 1986. Firms may choose to fund property, plant, and equipment off the balance sheet as a way of capturing *part* of the otherwise-lost tax shields. The portion that cannot be captured is a real cost. This may lead excess foreign tax credit firms to underinvest, to grow more slowly, and to restrict the scope of foreign operations; this behavior, in turn, reduces their needs for debt financing. The tax-law change may also skew investments by affected firms away from businesses in which the tax deductions are crucial to be competitive. In this way, the loss of U.S. multinational tax shields could represent substantial firm-specific costs.

One way to distinguish these possibilities is to examine changes in foreign and domestic operations after 1986. Firms that are unable to finance costlessly around the tax change face higher costs of holding foreign assets after 1986, since high ratios of foreign to domestic assets reduce interest tax deductions on outstanding debt. The results reported in Froot and Hines 1995 indicate that firms affected by the change in interest allocation rules scaled back their foreign operations in response. The affected firms also reduced the size of their total (domestic plus foreign) operations. Since there is no reason to expect these reactions from firms with access to low-cost substitutes for debt, this evidence indicates that the 1986 act imposed significant costs on firms with excess foreign tax credits.

---

18. Operating leases (to which we refer) are not included on the balance sheet, and the associated lease payments are fully deductible against U.S. taxable income. Capital leases, on the other hand, *are* included on the balance sheet, and their associated lease payments are (as is true of debt) allocated for tax purposes between domestic and foreign sources by section 861-8. We use measures of investment that include changes in capital leases but not in operating leases, and it is operating leases that are preferred by firms unable to take full advantage of lease tax deductions. See, for example, Smith and Wakeman 1985; Edwards and Mayer 1991.

9.4 Conclusion

The financing and investment patterns of American multinational firms reveal evidence of recent changes in the interest allocation rules. Specifically, the loss of full tax deductibility of parent-company interest expenses appears to have significantly reduced borrowing and investment by multinational firms with excess foreign tax credits. These results are consistent with the hypothesis that firms substitute away from debt when it becomes more expensive, as well as the hypothesis that the loss of interest tax deductibility increases a firm's cost of capital.

References

Altshuler, Rosanne, and Jack Mintz. 1994. U.S. Interest Allocation Rules: Effects and Policy. NBER Working Paper no. 4712. Cambridge, MA: National Bureau of Economic Research, April.

Collins, Julie H., and Douglas A. Shackleford. 1992. Foreign Tax Credit Limitations and Preferred Stock Issuances. *Journal of Accounting Research* 30:103–23.

Edwards, J. S. S., and C. P. Mayer. 1991. Leasing, Taxes, and the Cost of Capital. *Journal of Public Economics* 44:173–97.

Froot, Kenneth A., and James R. Hines, Jr. 1995. Interest Allocation Rules, Financing Patterns, and the Operations of U.S. Multinationals. In *The Effects of Taxation on Multinational Corporations,* ed. Martin Feldstein, James R. Hines, Jr., and R. Glenn Hubbard. Chicago: University of Chicago Press.

Gordon, Roger H., and Burton G. Malkiel. 1981. Corporation Finance. In *How Taxes Affect Economic Behavior,* ed. Henry J. Aaron and Joseph A. Pechman. Washington, DC: Brookings.

Lyon, Andrew B., and Gerald Silverstein. 1995. The Alternative Minimum Tax and the Behavior of Multinational Corporations. In *The Effects of Taxation on Multinational Corporations,* ed. Martin Feldstein, James R. Hines, Jr., and R. Glenn Hubbard. Chicago: University of Chicago Press.

Miller, Merton H. 1977. Debt and Taxes. *Journal of Finance* 32:261–75.

Scholes, Myron S., and Mark A. Wolfson. 1992. *Taxes and Business Strategy: A Planning Approach.* Englewood Cliffs, NJ: Prentice Hall.

Smith, Clifford W., Jr., and L. MacDonald Wakeman. 1985. Determinants of Corporate Leasing Policy. *Journal of Finance* 40:895–908.

Stiglitz, Joseph E. 1973. Taxation, Corporate Finance Policy, and the Cost of Capital. *Journal of Public Economics* 2:1–34.

10 International Accounting, Asymmetric Information, and Firm Investment

Jason G. Cummins, Trevor S. Harris, and Kevin A. Hassett

Policymakers generally assume that any tax breaks given to constituents will be taken. This seems a natural assumption, since, from the taxpayers' perspective, failure to claim a credit is akin to throwing away money. Unless we have some reason to believe that taxpayers are ignorant about the credit, we should expect them to claim it. It turns out that there is an important exception to this general rule. In this paper, we present evidence that many foreign firms act as if there is some cost to claiming tax credits or deductions. We argue that this may have an important impact on our understanding of the effects of corporate tax policy in an international setting.

It is natural to assume that minimizing tax payments is always optimal for the firm. For U.S. firms, it has generally been the case that they have no reason to avoid taking tax deductions or credits. There was, however, at least one episode when this was not true. Indeed, some firms purposely inflated their tax payments. A quick summary of this episode will make clear the relevant forces.

U.S. firms can account for inventory for tax purposes in many ways, with the two most prominent methods being the last-in-first-out (LIFO) and first-in-first-out (FIFO) systems. Firms are not required to actually manage their inventories in the way that they account for them for tax purposes, so they should choose whichever method leads to the lowest tax calculation. If there is inflation, a firm should calculate its profits for tax purposes using LIFO, since the most recently purchased good will be the most expensive, and the difference between sale price and cost will be the smallest. In the 1970s, how-

Jason G. Cummins is assistant professor of economics at New York University and John M. Olin Fellow at Columbia University. Trevor S. Harris is the Kester and Byrnes Professor of Accounting at the Graduate School of Business of Columbia University. Kevin A. Hassett is an economist at the Board of Governors of the Federal Reserve System. This paper does not necessarily reflect the views or opinions of the Board of Governors of the Federal Reserve.

Cummins and Harris acknowledge the financial support of the Center for International Business Education and Research and the Chazen Institute at Columbia University.

ever, there was one catch. If a firm used LIFO to calculate its taxable income, then it was required to use LIFO when calculating its accounting profits.[1] Accounting profits are reported to the Securities and Exchange Commission (SEC), and are used by stock-market participants (who never see the actual tax returns of firms) to value companies. Generally speaking, in the United States the methods used to calculate accounting profits are completely separate from those used to calculate taxes. There is a good reason for this: the rules that lead to the most informative signal to the stock market of the prospects of the firm may not be the same rules that lead to the most reliable enforcement of the tax code. For LIFO, this separation was violated, leading to a peculiar result. Firms sometimes chose to use FIFO instead of LIFO when valuing inventories. The most reasonable explanation for this choice is that using LIFO lowered taxes by lowering reported profits, and by shifting to LIFO firms might inadvertently signal lower profitability to the stock market. Presumably wary of large stock declines, firms used FIFO even though this increased total taxes paid to the U.S. Treasury (see Shoven and Bulow 1975).

The LIFO example provides a useful introduction to the discussion of multinational taxation because, for many countries, conformity between the tax and accounting books is the rule rather than the exception. In these countries, firms do not have to prepare separate tax and accounting reports. Just as conformity led some U.S. firms to choose not to use LIFO, it may be that firms based in "tax-conformity" or "one-book" countries will choose not to take advantage of many tax allowances and investment incentives. This could put them at a disadvantage relative to firms from "two-book" countries like the United States, where accounting and tax information are separate. Ignoring tax conformity when estimating the effects of taxes on multinational investment may provide very misleading inferences.

Obtaining knowledge of these effects is becoming increasingly important. The array of tax rates and rules facing a typical multinational firm is daunting. However, these complex rules present multinationals from most countries with strong locational incentives. For example, an investment tax credit (ITC) in the United States not only encourages U.S. firms to increase their investment; it also may attract investors from foreign countries. If the United States were considering the reinstitution of the ITC, policymakers would need to know how much additional investment it would induce. A substantial amount of research has evaluated the responses of firm investment to tax credits, so the analyst might be tempted to use some estimates from this literature to try to predict the effects of a credit. Even if the domestic response estimates were very precise, the analyst would probably be incorrect. This is because foreign corporations account for a sizable portion of investment in the United States,

---

1. Presently, there are footnotes in annual reports that contain the information shareholders would need to evaluate the impact of inventory valuation methods on reported profits.

and, for a number of reasons, we should expect them to react differently to U.S. tax policy than do domestic firms.

Foremost among these reasons is that income earned in the United States by foreign investors is subject to one of two home-country tax systems. Under a territorial system, the home country exempts income earned in the United States from home-country tax. Under a worldwide system, the home country taxes multinationals on their worldwide income. For an example of why this distinction is important, consider the case of a foreign multinational taxed on a worldwide basis, with its only foreign operations in the United States. Generally, U.S. taxes paid are credited against its home tax liability. If the home-country tax burden is higher than in the United States (as is usually the case), then any taxes paid to the United States are irrelevant, since they do not alter the firm's total (sum of U.S. and home-country) tax liability. If the U.S. tax rate is raised (but the total burden is still less than that in the home country), the U.S. firm's liabilities are raised, while the foreign multinational's ultimate tax payment is unchanged. Thus, a simple increase in the corporate tax rate benefits these foreign firms relative to U.S. firms.

Whether these forces impact capital flows is an important policy question. To date, researchers have related foreign direct investment to tax rates in many different countries and discovered that investment seems to respond to changes in taxes, although substantial uncertainty remains as to the size of these effects. This research has followed a long tradition by building upon models wherein firms equate the marginal revenue of investment to its marginal cost. The tax environment enters the decision to the extent that it alters either side of that equation. An ITC, for example, lowers the cost of each unit of capital.

In our present research, we argue that this last step, while usually appropriate when analyzing U.S. firms, may be inappropriate when studying multinational firms. As we argued above, many foreign multinationals exist in an environment where it is not always optimal for the decision makers to choose to minimize their taxes. Normal marginal cost–marginal revenue trade-offs do not apply for these firms because they operate in a different regulatory environment. Any empirical work that fails to account for this difference will be misleading.

The accounting environments in which firms operate generally fall into two classes. While the individual accounting practices differ in certain respects, the two systems that represent the ends of the conceptual spectrum are the German system (which is one-book) and the American system (which is two-book). To capture the core differences, we briefly outline these two benchmark regimes.

Figure 10.1 summarizes the basic organization of the U.S. system. In the United States, a firm aggregates information received from its subsidiaries into a consolidated tax return. The rules for constructing the return are designed by the tax authority, and reflect various policy objectives. At the same time, the parent firm provides a consolidated financial report for its shareholders that is

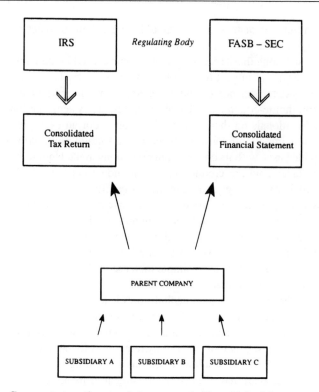

Fig. 10.1   Corporate taxation regulatory organization: United States

filed with the SEC. The rules that govern the construction of this report are designed to provide useful valuation information to stakeholders. Of course, accurate information about taxes is important for evaluating the profitability of the firm. For this purpose, the consolidated financial statements provide detailed footnotes about net tax expenses and liabilities.

Figure 10.2 summarizes the basic organization of the German system. All reporting is based on the Commercial Code. Each subsidiary files a separate, unconsolidated tax return with the Ministry of Finance, as does the parent. This is the first key difference from the two-book system. In Germany, tax law applies at the level of the "legal entity," not to the entire consolidated company. For example, losses by one branch of a company can usually not be used to offset profits elsewhere in the group (subject to certain profit-sharing conditions). The Ministry of Finance can also alter accounting rules via the tax law. Tax rules can feed back into the reporting practice via the "reverse authoritative principle," which requires firms to use tax rules when constructing their financial reports if no relevant rules exist in the Commercial Code. The parent also prepares a consolidated statement to present to its shareholders. This group report is based on reports from the individual legal entities. Historically, the

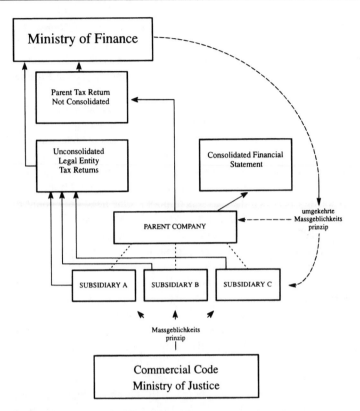

Fig. 10.2   Corporate taxation regulatory organization: Germany
Note: Umgekehrte Massgeblichkeits prinzip means reverse authoritative principle;
Massgeblichkeits prinzip means authoritative principle.

rules governing the construction of this statement have been, except for the consolidation itself, generally the same as those applying to the construction of the tax return. Hence, German companies exist in an environment similar to that faced by U.S. firms in the LIFO case. Maneuvering recorded in the tax return to lower tax liabilities shows up in the individual entity financial statements, and hence usually in the consolidated statements as well. Since this constraint caused U.S. firms to leave tax benefits unused, it is an interesting empirical question whether German companies tend to do the same.

The German system epitomizes one-book countries, but the classification of countries into one-book and two-book is something of an art. As we have explained, even the United States has features of its tax code that make it look like a one-book country. While the definitions are not dichotomous, we can map out a rough continuum of countries that fall between the United States and Germany. Countries that are largely two-book are Australia, Canada, Ireland, the Netherlands, New Zealand, the United Kingdom, and the United

States. Countries that are largely one-book include: Belgium, Denmark, France, Germany, Italy, Japan, Norway, Spain, Switzerland, and Sweden. While the majority of countries are one-book, as more countries seek to access international capital markets more countries are moving toward the two-book system.

To study whether there are behavioral differences between firms based in one- and two-book countries, we did detailed research on each of the above countries' systems, using the Global Vantage database, which contains, among other things, information on the investment decisions of firms in the seventeen countries we consider, over a period of twelve years (Cummins, Harris, and Hassett 1994). In the U.S. case, it was easy to identify the effects of information conformity between the two sets of books. One need only count the number of firms not using LIFO that would benefit from the switch (see Shoven and Bulow 1975). In the international setting, the problem is more difficult. Given the tangled web of tax codes, identification of the optimal tax strategy with respect to specific deductions is virtually impossible without having access to the firm's tax returns. There is an alternative, however. Many of the countries in our sample periodically change their corporate tax systems. As is the case in the United States, the value of depreciation deductions is frequently altered, and ITCs are switched on and off. These changes allow us to construct an experiment that identifies whether firms in one-book countries sometimes fail to claim available tax credits.

In our paper (1994), we develop a model that shows that one important implication of enforcing conformity between the tax and accounting books is that firms will behave as if they face an additional cost every time the firm claims a tax deduction. That is, to the extent that taking a tax benefit lowers reported income, tax benefits can hamper a firm's ability to signal profitability to the market, and may even signal a reduction in profits. Thus, when judging whether to invest and claim a tax deduction or credit, a firm must consider the extra "signaling" cost incurred if there is a risk that a "bad" signal will be sent to the market. We use the variation in investment policy across countries to ascertain whether firms in one-book countries behave as if they face an additional cost when responding to domestic investment tax incentives relative to two-book firms. For example, when an ITC is introduced in the United States, domestic firms increase their investment a certain amount. If Germany were to introduce an ITC identical to the one introduced in the United States, our theoretical analysis suggests that German firms would respond less to the increase than did the U.S. firms, because the German firms face the extra "signaling" cost. This study of the domestic response is an important precursor to an analysis of the specific effects of accounting regime on foreign capital flows. If one-book firms do not respond to tax credits in their own country, it is likely that credits from other countries will lead to little stimulus as well.

In our empirical analysis, we find that the one-book, two-book distinction is important when evaluating firms' responses to changes in domestic tax policy.

Roughly speaking, we find that firms in one-book countries respond about half as much to changes in tax policy as do firms in two-book countries. This means that, for example, an ITC of about 5 percent in the United States will induce about the same amount of extra investment as a 10 percent ITC in a one-book country. All told, this means that in addition to controlling for the worldwide-territorial distinction when evaluating the winners and losers with respect to current tax policy, it is important to control for the home accounting regime as well. Our estimates suggest that the extra "signaling" costs borne by firms in one-book countries are substantial, and tax changes that appear to advantage them may well be—as would be the case if the benefits to LIFO were improved slightly in the United States—inconsequential. In future research, we will expand upon this hypothesis and explore whether historical capital flows between countries can be better understood by applying these new insights.

References

Cummins, Jason G., Trevor S. Harris, and Kevin A. Hassett. 1994. Accounting standards, information flow, and firm investment behavior. NBER Working Paper no. 4685. Cambridge, MA: National Bureau of Economic Research, March.

Shoven, John B., and Jeremy I. Bulow. 1975. Inflation accounting and nonfinancial corporate profits: Physical assets. *Brookings Papers on Economic Activity,* 75 (March): 557–611.

Appendix

James R. Hines, Jr., and R. Glenn Hubbard

Most of the papers in this volume examine the impact of U.S. tax rules on the behavior of multinational corporations. Since reference to certain rather detailed aspects of the U.S. tax system occurs repeatedly in these papers, this appendix describes two of the major features of U.S. taxation of its resident multinational companies: how firms can defer U.S. taxation of certain foreign earnings, and how to determine whether an American company has "excess foreign tax credits."

The United States taxes income on a residence basis, meaning that American corporations and individuals owe taxes to the U.S. government on all their worldwide income, whether earned inside or outside the United States. In order to avoid subjecting American multinationals to double taxation, U.S. law permits firms to claim foreign tax credits for income taxes (and related taxes) paid to foreign governments.[1] The U.S. corporate tax rate is currently 35 percent. Under the foreign tax credit system, a U.S. corporation that earns $100 in a foreign country with a 15 percent tax rate pays a tax of $15 to the foreign government and $20 to the U.S. government, since its U.S. corporate tax liability of $35 (35 percent of $100) is reduced to $20 by the foreign tax credit of $15.

Deferral of U.S. Taxation

Under U.S. law, Americans must pay tax to the U.S. government on their worldwide incomes, except for a certain category of foreign income that is

---

1. The U.S. government is not alone in taxing the worldwide income of its resident companies while permitting firms to claim foreign tax credits. Other countries with such systems include Canada, Italy, Japan, Norway, and the United Kingdom. Under U.S. law, firms may claim foreign tax credits for taxes paid by foreign affiliates of which they own at least 10 percent, and only those taxes that qualify as income taxes are creditable.

temporarily excluded from U.S. taxation. The excluded category is the unrepatriated portion of the profits earned by foreign subsidiaries; taxpayers are permitted to defer any U.S. tax liabilities on those profits until those profits are paid as dividends to the United States.[2] This deferral is available only on the active business profits of American-owned foreign affiliates that are separately incorporated as subsidiaries in foreign countries. The profits of unincorporated foreign businesses, such as those of U.S.-owned branch banks in other countries, are taxed immediately by the United States.

To illustrate deferral, consider the case of a U.S.-owned subsidiary that earns $500 in a foreign country with a 10 percent tax rate. This subsidiary pays taxes of $50 to the foreign country (10 percent of $500), and might remit $100 in dividends to its parent U.S. company, using the remaining $350 ($500 − $50 of taxes − $100 of dividends) to reinvest in its own foreign operations. The U.S. parent firm must then pay U.S. taxes based on the $100 of dividends it receives (and is eligible to claim a foreign tax credit for the foreign income taxes its subsidiary paid on the $100). But the U.S. firm is not required to pay U.S. taxes on any part of the $350 that the subsidiary earns abroad and does not remit to its parent U.S. company. If, however, the subsidiary were to pay a dividend of $350 the following year, the firm would then be required to pay U.S. tax on that amount (after proper allowance for foreign tax credits).

U.S. tax law contains provisions designed to prevent American firms from delaying the repatriation of lightly taxed foreign earnings. These tax provisions apply to controlled foreign corporations, which are foreign corporations owned at least 50 percent by U.S. corporations or individuals holding stakes of at least 10 percent each. Under the subpart F provisions of U.S. law, certain types of the foreign income of controlled foreign corporations are "deemed distributed" and are therefore immediately taxable by the United States, even if not repatriated as dividend payments to American parent firms. This subpart F income can be from passive investments (such as interest and dividends received from investments in securities), foreign base company income (which arises from using a foreign affiliate as a conduit for certain types of international transactions), income that is invested in U.S. property, money used offshore to insure risks in the United States, and money used to pay bribes to foreign government officials. American firms with foreign subsidiaries that earn profits through most types of active business operations and that subsequently reinvest those profits in active lines of business are not subject to the subpart F rules, and are therefore able to defer U.S. tax liability on their foreign profits until they choose to remit dividends at a later date.

2. Deferral of home-country taxation of the unrepatriated profits of foreign subsidiaries is a common feature of systems that tax foreign incomes. Other countries that permit this kind of deferral include Canada, Denmark, France, Germany, Japan, Norway, Pakistan, and the United Kingdom.

Excess Foreign Tax Credits

The U.S. government permits American firms to claim foreign tax credits, with the understanding that this policy reduces the tax revenue collected by the United States on any given amount of foreign-source income. The foreign tax credit is intended to reduce the problems created by international double taxation. Consequently, the U.S. government is careful to design the foreign tax credit in a way that prevents American firms from using foreign tax credits to reduce U.S. tax liabilities that arise from profits earned *within* the United States.

The government imposes limits on the foreign tax credits that U.S. firms can claim; a firm's foreign tax credit limit equals the U.S. tax liability generated by the firm's foreign-source income. For example, with a U.S. tax rate of 35 percent, an American firm with $200 of foreign income faces a foreign tax credit limit of $70 (35 percent of $200). If the firm pays foreign income taxes of less than $70, then the firm would be entitled to claim foreign tax credits for all of its foreign taxes paid. If, however, the firm pays $95 of foreign taxes, it would be permitted to claim no more than $70 of foreign tax credits.

Firms described by this second case, in which foreign tax payments exceed the foreign tax credit limit, are said to have excess foreign tax credits; the excess foreign tax credits represent the portion of their foreign tax payments that exceeds the U.S. tax liabilities generated by their foreign incomes. Firms described by the first case, in which foreign tax payments are less than the foreign tax credit limit, are said to have excess foreign tax limitation.[3] Under U.S. law, firms can, under some circumstances, use excess foreign tax credits in one year to reduce their tax obligations for other years. Firms are allowed to apply any excess foreign tax credits against their U.S. tax obligations for up to the two previous years, and to recalculate their tax returns for those years while choosing when to apply the excess foreign tax credits. If a firm prefers, it can instead apply its excess foreign tax credits against U.S. tax liabilities on foreign income in up to the following five years.[4]

In practice, the calculation of the foreign tax credit limit entails many complications not addressed here. One major feature of the calculation should, however, be noted: U.S. law requires firms to use all of their worldwide foreign

3. An equivalent phrase used to describe firms with excess foreign tax limitation is to say that they have deficit foreign tax credits. These two phrases are used interchangeably.

4. Foreign tax credits are not adjusted for inflation, so firms generally find them to be the most valuable if claimed as soon as possible. Barring unusual circumstances, firms apply their foreign tax credits against future years only when they are unable to apply them against either of the previous two years. The most common reason for inability to apply excess foreign tax credits is that a firm already has excess foreign credits in those two years.

income to calculate the foreign tax credit limit. Firms then have excess foreign tax credits if the sum of their worldwide foreign income tax payments exceed this limit.[5] This procedure is known as worldwide averaging.

5. Not all countries that grant foreign tax credits use worldwide averaging. For example, while Japan uses worldwide averaging, the United Kingdom requires its firms to calculate foreign tax credits on an activity-by-activity basis. The United States used to require firms to calculate separate foreign tax credit limits for each country to which taxes were paid; the current system of worldwide averaging was introduced in the mid-1970s.

Contributors

Rosanne Altshuler
Department of Economics
New Jersey Hall
Rutgers University
New Brunswick, NJ 08903

Jason G. Cummins
Department of Economics
New York University
269 Mercer Street, Seventh Floor
New York, NY 10003

Martin Feldstein
NBER
1050 Massachusetts Avenue
Cambridge, MA 02138

Kenneth A. Froot
Graduate School of Business
Soldiers Field
Harvard University
Boston, MA 02163

Roger H. Gordon
Department of Economics
University of Michigan
Ann Arbor, MI 48109

Trevor S. Harris
Graduate School of Business
Uris Hall 610
Columbia University
New York, NY 10027

Kevin A. Hassett
Division of Research and Statistics
Board of Governors of the Federal
    Reserve System
Washington, DC 20551

James R. Hines, Jr.
NBER
1050 Massachusetts Avenue
Cambridge, MA 02138

R. Glenn Hubbard
Graduate School of Business
Uris Hall 609
Columbia University
New York, NY 10027

Joosung Jun
Department of Economics
Ewha University
Daihyun-dong, Seodaimun-ku
Seoul, Korea

Robert E. Lipsey
NBER
269 Mercer Street, Eighth Floor
New York, NY 10003

Andrew B. Lyon
Department of Economics
University of Maryland
College Park, MD 20742

Jeffrey K. MacKie-Mason
Department of Economics
University of Michigan
462 Lorch Hall
Ann Arbor, MI 48109

T. Scott Newlon
Office of Tax Analysis/5117
Department of the Treasury
Main Treasury Building
Washington, DC 20220

William C. Randolph
Congressional Budget Office
Second and D Street SW, Room 422
Washington, DC 20515

Gerald Silverstein
Office of Tax Analysis
Department of the Treasury
Main Treasury Building
Washington, DC 20220

Author Index

Subject Index

Accounting systems: last-in-first-out (LIFO) and first-in-first-out (FIFO), 95–96; one-book and two-book, 97–101

Alternative minimum tax (AMT): determinants of liability for, 40–41; incentives for income repatriation under, 43, 45–48; incentives in corporate, 3, 42–44, 49; rules of, 39; tax treatment of interest expense with, 83; U.S. tax paid on foreign income under, 43

Averaging, worldwide, 106

Borrowing. *See* Debt, foreign-source

Capital: conditions for leasing as opposed to owning, 90–92; influence of domestic and foreign tax rules on cost of, 21–22; mobility, 17, 35. *See also* Cost of capital

Capital budget investment allocation, 16–17

Capital flows: cross-border financing of foreign affiliates, 17–18; cross-border flow with FDI, 17–18; gross and net international, 15; impact of global tax policies, 97

Capital market, segmented global, 15–16

Corporate tax. *See* Taxation

Corporations. *See* Firms; Multinational corporations (MNCs)

Cost of capital: defined, 22; with dividend repatriation tax price changes, 78; foreign investment financed by local borrowing, 26–27; influence of taxes on, 21; methodology to calculate, 23; for multinational

firms in Japan, 24–25; for U.S. and local firms in foreign markets, 23–24

Data sources: analysis of firm behavior under different accounting systems, 100–101; analysis of MNC reaction to tax reform (1986), 87–88; for dividend repatriation analysis, 68–69; of multinational firm R&D, 57–59; outbound FDI, 74, 77

Debt: differences in effect of domestic and foreign borrowing, 18–19; foreign-based local, 26–27

Debt, foreign-source: as exchange risk hedge, 27; in financing of U.S. foreign affiliates, 17–18, 26; U.S. multinational, 14–18. *See also* Cost of capital; Interest expense

Discount rate, 22–23

Dividends, corporate: present value with FDI, 18–19; trapped-equity or tax-capitalization approach, 76n10

Dividends, foreign-source: cost of capital with credits for, 24–25; model of repatriation, 67–71; tax price of remittances, 64, 65–71, 78; variability of repatriation tax on, 64. *See also* Tax price

Employment, U.S. overseas affiliates, 8

Equity financing: foreign investment by U.S. foreign affiliates, 17–18; tax cost for U.S. firms, 27

Export markets, U.S. firms, 9–10, 12

Firms: AMT, 39–40; behavior under different